D0500646

Exceptional **Service,**
Exceptional **Profit**

Exceptional **Service,**
Exceptional **Profit**

The Secrets of Building a Five-Star Customer Service Organization

Leonardo Inghilleri
and Micah Solomon

Foreword by Horst Schulze

AMACOM

American Management Association
New York • Atlanta • Brussels • Chicago • Mexico City • San Francisco
Shanghai • Tokyo • Toronto • Washington, D.C.

Special discounts on bulk quantities of AMACOM books are
available to corporations, professional associations, and other
organizations. For details, contact Special Sales Department,
AMACOM, a division of American Management Association,
1601 Broadway, New York, NY 10019.
Tel: 800-250-5308. Fax: 518-891-2372.
E-mail: specialsls@amanet.org
Website: www.amacombooks.org/go/specialsales
To view all AMACOM titles go to: www.amacombooks.org

This publication is designed to provide accurate and authoritative
information in regard to the subject matter covered. It is sold with the
understanding that neither the publisher nor the authors are engaged in
rendering legal, accounting, or other professional service. If legal advice
or other expert assistance is required, the services of a competent
professional person should be sought.

In a few instances the authors have concealed identifying characteristics of individuals and businesses,
especially in less-than-laudatory examples. Also, the fictitious brand names DinoFuels, TapasTree,
L&M Stagers, Kiddie Carousel, Stutterfly, and Swirly Goo and the Goners are used only for humor
and should not be confused with similarly named or configured companies.

Copyrights for Appendices are as follows:
Appendix A: © Four Aces Inc., courtesy of Micah Solomon, All Rights Reserved
Appendix B: © General Parts, Inc., All Rights Reserved
Appendix C: © West Paces Hotel Group, All Rights Reserved

Library of Congress Cataloging-in-Publication Data

Inghilleri, Leonardo.
  Exceptional service, exceptional profit : the secrets of building a five-star customer service
organization / Leonardo Inghilleri and Micah Solomon.
      p.   cm.
  Includes index.
  ISBN-13: 978-0-8144-1538-2
  ISBN-10: 0-8144-1538-5
  1. Customer service.   2. Consumer satisfaction.   3. Customer loyalty.   I. Solomon,
Micah.   II. Title.

  HF5415.5.I543   2010
  658.8'12—dc22
                                                                    2009031674

© 2010 Leonardo Inghilleri and Micah Solomon
All rights reserved.
Printed in the United States of America.

This publication may not be reproduced, stored in a retrieval system, or transmitted in whole or in part,
in any form or by any means, electronic, mechanical, photocopying, recording, or otherwise, without
the prior written permission of AMACOM, a division of American Management Association, 1601
Broadway, New York, NY 10019.

Printing number

10   9   8   7

Contents

Chapter Four:
Recovery! Turning Service Failures Around 26

Chapter Five:
Keeping Track to Bring Them Back: Tracking Customer Roles, Goals, and Preferences 45

Chapter Six:
Building Anticipation *Into* Your Products and Services: Putting Processes to Work for You 59

Chapter Seven:
Your People: Selection, Orientation, Training, and Reinforcement 84

Chapter Eleven:
Hello/Good-Bye: Two Crucial Moments with a Customer 131

Appendixes 145

Appendix A:
Oasis Disc Manufacturing: Customer and Phone Interaction Guidelines and Lexicon Excerpts 147

Appendix B:
CARQUEST Standards of Service Excellence 153

Appendix C:
Capella Hotels and Resorts "Canon Card": Service Standards and Operating Philosophy 155

Notes 159

Index 163

Special Features

Acknowledgments

I dedicate this book to all those service professionals who provide us with memorable experiences that enrich and brighten our daily lives.

I wish to thank my lovely wife Solange, whose patience and unconditional support have allowed me to pursue my professional goals and aspirations. For the past twenty-three years, Solange's wisdom and matter-of-fact view of life have kept me grounded on Planet Earth and have provided a sounding board for my ideas and concepts. I wish also to thank my wonderful sons, Gianluca and Niccoló (and not least for sharing their unique perspective on what is *cool* and what is *not!*).

I also wish to thank Horst Schulze—my "boss," friend, mentor, and partner—who taught me *everything* I needed to know about exceptional customer service. Horst's laser-sharp focus on excellence and his unmatched commitment to being the best have been both an inspiration and a motivation to succeed.

And finally, I want to thank my friend Micah, whose bright and witty style brings a wonderful dimension to the business concepts we present together in these pages; I had a great time writing this book with him.

Leonardo Inghilleri
Atlanta, Georgia

To my beloved and brilliant wife, my family, my friends, my colleagues past and present at Oasis, Tony, Morris, and the team at AVL, and my customers: You have taught me so well and patiently—enduring my failings over the years while I learned what is contained in these pages.

To my smarter-than-me brother, Ari Solomon; our wise and accommodating editor Bob Nirkind and the team at AMACOM; super-agent Bill Gladstone; Gareth Branwyn; Tom Burdette; Seth Godin; Richard Isen; Cathy Mosca; Rajesh Setty; the people at ChangeThis/800-CEO-READ; Rick Wolff and Caryn Karmatz Rudy; Megan Pincus Kajitani (for "Jane Chang-Katzenberg" [Chapter 3]); and, most of all, Leonardo: This book would not have happened without you.

Thank you all—so much.

Micah Solomon
Philadelphia, PA

Foreword

So-called Customer Relationship Management prides itself on volume, on speed, on "efficiency." This might sound good on paper, but what truly matters, what builds strategic value for a business, is loyalty: customer loyalty, employee loyalty. Without knowing the secrets to building these, even innovative companies struggle. They can massage data all they like; they can profile large groups of customers all they like. Do they empower their employees to use judgment in any real sense? If not, the employees will leave when they sense a dead end. Customers, shareholders, and other stakeholders will ultimately prove to be short-timers as well, no matter how innovative and admirable the products and services offered.

Actual service, from someone who offers a caring face and a helping hand, is a universal desire. Learning how to achieve it, though, is far from universally understood. The problem is that these principles are not always easy and often go against the grain of modern business practices, and you need someone to show you the way.

That's where this book comes in. *Exceptional Service, Exceptional Profit* is the first book to describe comprehensively the principles that assisted us in winning two Malcolm Baldrige awards at The Ritz-Carlton and now guide us at our Capella and Solis hotel brands. These are the principles we also employ with our West Paces Consulting clients in a wide variety of industries, from food service to auto parts.

Also unique to this volume is the high-tech, bootstrapping twenty-first century perspective of Micah Solomon, known for his unusual achievements in entrepreneurship and service.

The principles on which we base our hospitality approach are pulled from a rich background. Some reflect back to information as old as Adam Smith, most clearly in our feelings about employee relations and training. Many others reference well-established concepts—ideas from Deming, Juran, and Crosby—but in a new framework.

The way these concepts are molded together is groundbreaking. What you read here will allow you to recalibrate your business, on any scale, to replicate the exceptional but small-scale achievement of the idealized sole proprietor archetype: to truly know your customers and keep them coming back for more.

These perspectives are revolutionary. And they aren't for everyone.

When we say that the CEO should personally conduct orientation, we mean it. When we say it's deadly to cheapen your product in ways that matter to your customer, we mean it. When we say you need to take the customer's position quickly, or you might as well not take it at all, we mean it. When we say that you serve but you are not a servant, we mean it. These are revolutionary statements, and you will benefit from a service revolution in your own management world and in the bottom line. Thank you for reading.

Horst Schulze
Chairman and CEO, The West Paces Hotel Group
President and COO (retired) The Ritz-Carlton Hotel Company

Exceptional **Service,**
Exceptional **Profit**

The Only Shop in the Marketplace

The best thing you can do for your business right now has nothing to do with new technology, economies of scale, or first-mover advantage.

It's something simpler.

It's something more dependable.

The single best thing you can do for your business is to build true customer loyalty, one customer at a time.

Everything changes when a customer becomes a loyalist. To the truly loyal customer, you are the only shop in the marketplace. All the other brands and all the other vendors don't even come into focus. Like someone in love, the loyal customer only has eyes for you.

Few businesses realize how valuable customer loyalty is, and even fewer know how to achieve it consistently. But a company of any size can build great wealth and stability through customer loyalty. Businesses with loyal customers grow faster than others when times are good, and they have the most breathing room when times are bad.

At its root, creating loyal customers is about taking the time to learn about your customers individually and then using simple systems to turn that knowledge into enduring business relationships. In doing so, you turn your offering into much more than a commodity—you turn it into a personal relationship.

The primary threat to a business today is the perception by customers that all you offer is a replaceable, interchangeable commodity. This hazard stalks your every move: No matter how unbreachable your business's advantages may appear right now, whether they are advantages of technology, geography, or branding, eventually your business model *is* going to be knocked off. And, in this era of accelerating change, it will likely happen sooner than you think.

Escape this threat of commoditization by creating enduring, loyal, *human* relationships with customers. It's the surest way to escape market obsolescence.

The payoff is huge.

Learning to create loyal customers has made all the difference for the companies where Leonardo has been involved, including The Ritz-Carlton, BVLGARI, The Walt Disney Company, and the new hotel brands—Capella and Solis—that Leonardo heads up with his partners.

The principles that lead to loyal customers will work for you, too. They're simple, they're solid, and they're replicable. You needn't work in a luxury industry to apply them. Far from it.

As you'll learn, Micah used the principles of loyalty to transform a tiny manufacturing and entertainment services company he started in a single room in his basement, with financing that consisted of only a credit card, into a renowned and high-growth enterprise. His approach built his company, Oasis, into one of the top players in its field, as well as attracting attention in the business literature, including case studies in such places as *Success* magazine and Seth Godin's bestseller *Purple Cow.* Oasis catapulted to success because customers respond with loyalty when you treat them according to the principles and methods we will describe.

Since then, Leonardo and Micah have been able to lend their loyalty-based methodology to a great diversity of industries: from white shoe law firms to restaurants to banks to organic flower farms; from tour operators to independent music labels to convention centers to hospitals. Loyalty pays off—measurably—for all of them.

The reward for using these principles isn't only financial. As you begin building customer loyalty, your pride in your profession, your integrity, and your ability to build positive relationships (at work, and even in your own home) will also bloom. This happens naturally, because the process of earning loyalty involves caring about your customers, respecting them, and thinking constantly about their needs. Spending this time being deeply attentive will tone your personality.

Building customer loyalty will require your hard work and thoughtfulness, but it is a refreshingly straightforward process. While so many aspects of business are out of your control—exchange rates, international tension, technological changes—the single most important process, creating loyal customers, obeys predictable, stable rules that can be mastered and then applied successfully for a lifetime.

We're pleased to help show the way.

CHAPTER ONE

The Engineer on the Ladder

Reaching for the Highest Level of Service

Suppose you're the manager of a group of hotels. In one of them, a maintenance engineer is replacing a light bulb in the lobby ceiling. Out of the corner of his eye he notices a woman and her two sons coming from the pool, wrapped in towels but still dripping wet. The woman has her hands full with bags. She fumbles with the door that leads into the lobby, looking exasperated. The man on the ladder becomes alert to her predicament, puts down his tools, climbs down, crosses the lobby, smiles, and opens the door for her.

"Welcome back to the hotel, ma'am," he says. "Let me help you with your bags. How was the pool? Did your two little guys have a good time? What floor are you going to?" He presses the button, exits the elevator, and heads back toward his ladder.

When we spin this story out for executives and managers in our seminars, the most common first reaction is envy: "I'd be thrilled to have my rank and file achieve this level of customer service," runs a typical response. "The customer expressed a need, and 'my' employee responded energetically," says a manager. "He got off the ladder rather than saying 'That's not my job.' So what's not to like?"

It's true: We've all seen worse. But there's still plenty to dislike. As upbeat as this encounter was, it was reactive: The woman had to fumble with the door, thereby making her frustration known so the engineer would react. Reactive service is a pretty ineffective way to create loyal customers. To get on the fast track to customer loyalty, your company needs something better.

The magic happens when you, your systems, and the employees throughout the ranks of your business *anticipate* the needs of your customers, learning to recognize and respond to the needs of your customers before they are expressed—sometimes before your customers even realize they have a need. That is the difference between providing ho-hum service by merely reacting to customer requests and building loyalty through true *anticipatory* service.

Function Versus Purpose

Picture this instead: What if the moment your fellow on the ladder sees the overburdened mom returning from the pool, he thinks to himself, "My routine daily *function* is to change light bulbs, paint ceilings, and fix pipes, but the reason I'm here, *my purpose*, is to help create a memorable experience for guests"? Understanding this, he immediately climbs down and opens the door for her—*before* she has to fumble with the door handle or knock to get attention.

The maintenance engineer—inspired by your leadership—has now provided genuine service that *anticipates* the customer's needs. The timing of the engineer's intervention is the only measurable change, but what a difference that tiny change makes! Suddenly this employee has anticipated a customer's need, a need she has not yet expressed. In doing so, he has honored her idiosyncratic life circumstances—her individual humanity.

This extraordinary kind of service is a highly reliable path to winning customer loyalty. In the chapters ahead we will equip you to make such service encounters the rule rather than the exception, at all levels of your company.

You probably have doubts.

You may doubt that *your* maintenance engineer or other rank and file worker would ever anticipate the needs of customers so masterfully. We'll show you how and why he can and will.

You may doubt that you can afford to create such lavish standards of service. As one of our students put it, "In one of Leonardo's five-star resorts, I can see it, maybe. But in Micah's bootstrapped ventures—how does *he* pull off that level of service? As for my own company, I need my maintenance workers to stay up on their ladders, thank you very much!"

Actually, creating extraordinary service systems is a cost-effective proposition for almost any business: the natural outcome of a systematic approach to customers. And such service pays great dividends in reasonably short order.

First Steps First

Before we get to the creation of those all-important loyal customers through anticipatory service, we'd like to ensure you've pinned down a more basic initial step: creating simple customer satisfaction. We'll head there first.

CHAPTER TWO

The Four Elements of Customer Satisfaction

Perfect Product, Caring Delivery, Timeliness, and an Effective Problem Resolution Process

There's not much point in taking a specialized upper-level course before you've studied the field's introductory concepts. In a similar vein, there are prerequisites to meet before you can learn to provide extraordinary, loyalty-building customer service.

First, become adept at meeting the more fundamental expectations of your customers. That is, learn to make them *satisfied*.

What does a satisfied customer look like? She thinks your business offers a reasonable solution that it delivers well. If *asked*, she'll say nice things about you. But although she may have some warm feelings for your business, she's not yet an advocate for your brand, and, unlike a truly loyal customer, she can still be wooed away. A merely satisfied customer is still a free agent, exploring the marketplace.

She still has a wandering eye.

Nonetheless, simple customer satisfaction is one of the underpinnings of the exceptional relationship we call true customer loyalty. And, fortunately, customer satisfaction is based on four predictable factors. Customers are satisfied whenever they consistently receive:

1. A perfect product
2. Delivered by a caring, friendly person
3. In a timely fashion
    . . . with (because any of those three elements may misfire)
4. The support of an effective problem resolution process

A Perfect Product

Customers want defect-free products and services. You need to design your product or service so that it can be expected to function perfectly *within foreseeable boundaries.*

Things will sometimes go wrong. Your products, and people, will sometimes fail due to unpredictable circumstances. But sloppy or incomplete product or service design is, from a customer's perspective, intolerable.

Suppose you're staffing an online photo lab. Let's call it Stutterfly. You know from experience that one prepress technician (PPT) is needed for every 100 orders in-house. Now suppose you want to be ready for a maximum of 1,000 photo orders at any given time. How many prepress technicians do you need? Ten? Perhaps. But a "perfectly designed" answer needs to take into account absenteeism, last minute no-shows, and vacation time: any reasonably foreseeable scenario that could prevent you from actually having ten PPTs on hand to cover the orders in-house. In addition, your "perfect design" needs to include provisions for getting these technicians all the supplies, tools, resources, and information they'll need to do a great job.

Of course, something that is not realistically foreseeable could still happen: six of your ten PPTs might get the flu on the same night, or a major earthquake could knock a paper mill that supplies you out of commission. The product will not always be perfectly deliverable. We know.

But you must design it to be perfect—foreseeing all that is foreseeable.

Designing the Defects In

Obviously, getting planes in the air and to their destination is complex and filled with variables. Any reasonable passenger will understand that delivery of this "product" (like most things in today's marketplace, actually a combination of a service and a product) will be flawed from time to time. But that's no excuse for designing the flaws in. Ask the frequent travelers you know if anyone has experienced a single on-time departure out of LaGuardia Airport on a Friday afternoon after 5 p.m. (Maybe our luck is extraordinarily bad, but we're still waiting for our first one!) This service, in other words, is *designed to fail to function* within foreseeable boundaries.

Delivered by Caring People

Your perfect product now requires caring, friendly people to deliver it. Let's visualize just how a product and its delivery work together to determine satisfaction. Let's make the setting Hartsfield-Jackson International Airport in Atlanta. Picture featureless corridors, long ticket counters, and the reason you wish you didn't have to exchange your ticket a few days before Thanksgiving: a maze of people waiting behind a roped line to speak with any of five agents. Eventually, you make it to the front of the maze. Now you're first in line, waiting politely for an agent at the counter to help you.

What do you hear?

"Next!"

Hmmm. As you approach the agent, you see that her *"Next"* was premature.

So you stand there, waiting for her to finish the previous transaction.

Finally she finishes keyboarding, looks at you, and says curtly: *"Yes?"*

You answer, "My plans have changed. Would it be possible to exchange this ticket so I can fly to Washington Dulles?"

"Uh huh . . ."

She takes your ID, gives you your boarding pass—and never looks up at you.

"Next!"

You take the boarding pass, go through security, get on the plane, and land safely and on time at your destination. So, you got a perfect product: a product that would appear, if anyone charted it out, to be 100 percent free of defects.

But do you feel satisfied?

Of course not.

OK. Now let's change the script. Same airport, same maze, same line of people ahead of you in the maze. Again, you eventually make it to the front of the line, where you quietly wait for an agent to call on you.

"May I help the next person in line, please?" (You step forward.)

"Good morning, Sir. Thank you for your patience. How are you today?"

"Not bad at all, thanks, considering, and how are you?"

"Just fabulous. How may I assist you today?"

"My plans have changed, and I need to get on a flight to Washington Dulles."

"It'll be my pleasure. I hear the weather isn't actually too bad in the D.C. area this weekend. Are you visiting family for Thanksgiving?"

"No, it's just business. But I'll be flying back right afterward and will get home for the holiday." (She checks your ID and hands you your boarding pass.)

"Is there anything else I can do for you today?"

"No, I think that's all."

"Well then, have a splendid day."

"Thank you very much."

"Thank you for flying with us."

How was *this* interaction? It was great, right? An interaction like this, with just a single caring, friendly employee, can make us feel good about doing business with an entire company.

Now you get through the long security line and to the gate. Only at that point do you notice your boarding pass says *Dallas,* not Dulles.

Uh . . . *now* are you satisfied?

Again, no—not with a defective product or service, no matter how warmly delivered.

In a Timely Fashion

In our world of iPhones and IM, your customers get to decide what is and isn't an appropriate timeline. A perfect product delivered *late* by friendly, caring people *is the equivalent of a defective one.*

Customer experiences guide their expectations, so on-time delivery standards continue to get tougher all the time. What your customer today thinks of as on-time delivery is not only stricter than what her parents would have tolerated, it's stricter than what even her older sister would have tolerated.

Amazon.com's tight supply and delivery chain has single-handedly raised the timeliness bar in the online world, but that's not the end of the story: Their speedy online delivery has raised *offline* expectations as well. In fact, the concept of special ordering for walk-in customers is obsolete for most brick-and-mortar merchants. If you don't have it in stock when a customer walks in, a customer's just going to go online and find it for herself.

This impatience rule can only be disregarded when a customer is commissioning something truly custom, something specially made by you for her alone, such as fine art, cabinetry, or a gourmet meal. In fact, for some truly custom items, providing something *too quickly* can be equated by customers with low quality or prefab work. The trick here is the same: Learn your own customers' definition of "on time," and obey that definition—not your own.

Reset Customer Expectations You Can't Meet

Suppose you are a lawyer. Your client calls and leaves a request on your voicemail. Without comment, you begin the research your answer will require. Proudly—four days after the client's request—you submit your carefully crafted, well-researched opinion, only to find yourself talking to an irritated client! Why? What's the matter with this guy? Doesn't he understand how complex this issue is?

Well, actually, no. In your client's eyes, you are an expert in everything related to law, and it's his expectation that you'll respond to a request promptly. Instead, you took four days to get back to him.

With a better understanding of your client's expectations, you could have picked up the phone and made a call at the outset: "Hello, Bill. This is Jenny. Thank you for your request. It is a fairly complicated issue, and I'll need a couple of days to research it. I'll send you the opinion by the end of the week. Talk with you soon!" You could have taken the initiative, reset the expectation, and prevented the erosion of confidence and trust you've now suffered. You would have made him feel all the more grateful for your hard work when you eventually do call. This approach of setting clear expectations for deadlines is simple, yet curiously uncommon. Try it on for size.

With the Support of an Effective Problem Resolution Process

Service breakdowns and other problems experienced by customers are crucial emotional moments in a business relationship. Therefore, solving these problems will have an outsized impact on your business success. That's why you need an effective problem resolution process.

Effective problem resolution sounds like a modest goal. But so does reaching base camp—until you find out you're climbing Denali. A big reason it's so tough? *Effective* cannot be measured by whether you have restored the situation to the pre-problem status quo. *Effective* is measured by whether you have restored customer satisfaction.

This can be challenging, but it's well worth it. Resolve a service problem effectively and your customer is *more* likely to become loyal than if she'd never run into a problem in the first place. (On this point, our studies and practical experience are 100 percent conclusive.) Why is this so? *Because until a problem occurs, the customer doesn't get to see us fully strut our service.* Of course, we would never recommend that you make mistakes on purpose so you can engineer a splendid recovery and win yourself some client love in the process. But it is a silver lining to keep in mind when you're staring down a problem.

The topic of effective problem resolution, especially the handling of service breakdowns, is so crucial that it will fill all of Chapter Four. First though, we need to explore a fundamental tool: *language.* Because no matter what lengths you go to for your customers, if you don't use the right words with them, they'll never appreciate how good they have it. Language is crucial to how a customer experiences your business, which makes it a critical element of your brand. It's the next stop on our itinerary.

CHAPTER THREE

Language Engineering

Every. Word. Counts.

Your company has probably given more thought to the language it uses in marketing campaigns than to the words employees use when having conversations face-to-face with customers. That's a mistake, because customers don't generally get their make-or-break impressions of your company from high-minded branding exercises. They get them primarily from *day-to-day conversations with you.* And those are the impressions they spread to others.

Language underlies all other components of customer satisfaction. For example:

> ➤ A perfect product won't be *experienced* as perfect unless you also use the right language in describing it to customers.

> ➤ Even your most well-intentioned and technically flawless employees can alienate customers if they use the wrong language.

> ➤ When you have a service failure, the right words can be your best ally.

If you haven't given much thought to selecting and controlling your company language—what your staff, signage, emails, voicemails, and web-based autoresponders should say, and should *never* say, to customers—it's time to do it now.

Establish a Consistent Style of Speech

No brand is complete until a brand-appropriate style of speaking with customers is in place at all levels of the enterprise. You should therefore work to achieve a consistent style of service speech.

A distinctive and consistent companywide style of service speech won't happen on its own. You'll need social engineering: that is, systematic training of employees. Imagine, for example, that you've selected ten promising salespeople for your new high-end jewelry boutique. You've provided them with uniforms and stylish haircuts and encouraged them to become your own brand's versions of a Mr. or Ms. Cartier, starting on opening day. But they'll still speak with customers much the way they speak in their own homes: that is, until you've trained them in a different language style.

Happily, "engineering" a company-wide style of speech can be a positive, collaborative experience. If you approach this correctly, you won't need to put a gag on anybody or twist any arms. Once everybody in an organization understands the reasons for language guidelines, it becomes a challenge, not a hindrance. The improved customer reactions and collaborative pride of mission are rewarding. As a consequence, our clients have found it to be a pretty easy sell companywide.

Here's how to make it happen.

Create a Lexicon of Preferred Language and Phrasing

To help launch their Ritz-Carlton luxury hotel brand, initially, founding President and Chief Operating Officer Horst Schulze and his team decided on a set of ideal phrases for use in conversation with customers, then trained employees to use those phrases. The frequent use of certain phrases helped unify their employees around a shared identity and contributed to a distinctive "Ritz style" that the public could easily recognize: phrases like "My pleasure," "Right away," "Certainly," and—a personal favorite—"We're fully committed tonight." (Translation: "We're booked solid, bub!") The list of words and phrases to be avoided included *folks, hey, you guys,* and *okay.*

(It's easy in the 21st century to miss the conscious choices behind this, because a Ritz-style vocabulary now pervades the hospitality industry. This occurred for a few different reasons: through imitation by competitors, because it entered the public consciousness when the late William Safire and others in the mainstream press covered the phenomenon, and because Ritz-Carlton alumni have dispersed to other companies, carrying their Ritz language with them consciously or as second nature.)

We recommend you take an approach similar to The Ritz's, although not necessarily with their same English Country Manor overtones. Study the language that works best with your own customers, and identify harmful phrases that should be avoided. Codify this for your employees in a brief lexicon or language handbook that can be learned and referred to on the job. In the lexicon, you'll spell out which words and phrases are best to use and which should be avoided in various common situations.

Putting together a language handbook is a relatively simple undertaking. It doesn't require an English degree. But it does require forethought, experimentation, and some pondering about human nature. Here, for example, are some good/bad language choices Micah uses in the manual he developed for use in his business ventures (see Appendix for more examples and scenarios from his company Oasis):

Bad: "You owe . . ."
Good: "Our records show a balance of . . ."

Bad: "You need to . . ." *(This makes some customers think: "I don't* **need** *to do jack, buddy—I'm your customer!")*
Good: "We find it usually works best when . . ."

Bad: "Please hold."

Good: "May I briefly place you on hold?" *(and then actually* **listen** *to the caller's answer)*

Good lexicons will vary depending on industry, clientele, and location. A cheerful "No worries!" sounds fine coming from the clerk at a Bose audio store in Portland (an informal business in an informal town) but bizarre if spoken by the concierge at the Four Seasons in Milan.

Choose Language to Put Customers at Ease, Not to Dominate Them

No matter what your business is, make it your mission to avoid recommending any condescending or coercive language in your lexicon. Sometimes this kind of language is obvious, but sometimes it's quite subtle. Here are examples:

Subtly insulting: In an informal business, if a customer asks, "How are you?" the response, "I'm well," is grammatically correct—but may not be the best choice. Hearing this very "correct" response may make your customers momentarily self-conscious about their own potentially imperfect grammar. It may be better to have your employees choose from more familiar alternatives like, "I'm doing great!" or "Super!" (Most important, of course, is to follow up with an inquiry about the customer's *own* well-being: "And how are **you**, this morning?")

Unsubtly coercive: We're not likely to forget the famous steakhouse that trained staff to ask as they seated us, "Which bottled water will you be enjoying with us this evening, still, or sparkling?" We took that phrasing to mean we weren't permitted to ask for tap water.

(In this situation, one that comes up in nearly every restaurant, what *is* a better choice of words? How about: "Would you prefer ice water or bottled water with your meal?" Or, considering that this question offers an early chance for the waitstaff to build rapport with guests, add some local flavor. In Chicago, a friend's restaurant a few years back was asking, "Will you be having bottled water or Mayor Daley's finest aqua with your meal?")

We believe a Ritz-Carlton style "Say *This* While Avoiding *This*" language guide optimizes customer satisfaction in most businesses and helps bind staff members into a team. But if it strikes you as too prescriptive (or too much work) to develop scripted phrases and specific word choices for your employees, at least consider developing a brief "Negative Lexicon." A Negative Lexicon is just a list of crucial *Thou Shalt Nots*.

We call the Negative Lexicon the Danny Meyer approach, after the teachings of the New York restaurateur and master of hospitality. Meyer feels uncomfortable giving his staff a list of what *to* say, but he doesn't hesitate to specifically *ban* phrases that grate on his ears ("Are we still working on the lamb?")[1]

A Negative Lexicon can be kept short, sweet, and easy to learn. Of course, new problematic words and phrases are sure to crop up as time moves on. Ideally, you'll update your Negative Lexicon as frequently as *Wired* magazine updates its "Jargon Watch" column.

Concentrate Your Language Efforts on the Key Customer Moments: Hellos, Good-Byes, and the Times When Things Fall Apart

Concentrate your language efforts on the most vivid, emotionally crucial points in your conversations with customers. Social psychologists, notably Elizabeth Loftus, have proven that human memory radically simplifies our emotional experiences when it files them away for storage; our minds normally retain only the most vivid aspects from each situation, letting go of whatever else might have occurred.[2]

So focus your language efforts on moments that are known to remain vivid in memory: hellos (make yours unusually warm and personal), good–byes (make them wonderful), and recoveries after service failures (yours should be more graceful than anybody else's).

It's Not You. It's Them, *Plus* Their Background, *Plus* You

Psychologists find that two people listening to the exact same conversation can come away with completely different impressions of the people involved. You've probably noticed something like this in your workplace: You think your colleague Jim seems friendly and kind; Margaret thinks he's a suckup.

Why does this happen? *Cultural differences* are a big part of the story. Culture is the set of assumptions, traditions, and values a community develops over time. Thus, members of a culture other than yours may interpret your behavior in ways that haven't occurred to you, because of their community's own assumptions, traditions, or values. Cultural differences can create particularly bad impressions when you interact with a customer from a different part of the world—or even a subculture within your own country. To manage this risk, we recommend becoming expert on cultures your company serves and expert at cross-cultural communication in general. There are some superb books that can guide you, such as Brooks Peterson's *Cultural Intelligence: A Guide to Working with People from Other Cultures* (Intercultural Press, 2004).

A caution: Be sure to apply your new expertise *flexibly*. Individuals don't always subscribe to their culture's assumptions, norms, or values: Personality or family background can be a more powerful determinant of an individual's values. Over and over, you hear us recommend that you think about your customers as individuals rather than as groups. This core principle applies to cross-cultural communication, too.

Shut Up Sometimes: The Artie Bucco Principle

The tragicomic character on *The Sopranos*, Artie Bucco, starts the series as a successful restaurateur. Slowly, though, things begin to fall apart for him. Finally, his wife, Charmaine, has the painful job of telling him what is going so wrong: that his customers come to the restaurant to be with each other, not with him. Their special moments are for them, not for him, and interrupting them with what *he* thinks is important is driving them away. Artie never does get the message when he interacts with customers. If he had learned to listen between the lines, he could have picked it up, as his wife did.

She was listening.

Align your organization to the value of listening. Learn to adjust the flow of your comments to match each customer's interests and mood.

And practice shutting up sometimes.

Words Have Their Limits

Visual and physical cues can speak louder than words. Make sure your words aren't being contradicted by nonverbal messages, such as:

- ➤ Employees who say "Welcome" while their body language telegraphs "*Go away!*"

- ➤ First-point-of-contact employees whose chairs are oriented so their backs face arriving guests, or who, although oriented correctly, are so "efficiently" engaged in computer tasks that they may as well not be placed at a greeting location at all.

- ➤ An office building with obstructed ramps or heavy, hard-to-open doors. (What does that "say" to a customer who is in a wheelchair, has arthritis, or is pushing a stroller?)

- ➤ Small items kept under lock and key in a way that silently insults your customers: for example, a corkscrew that is locked down with a security chain to prevent its theft—at a four star hotel?!

It's true—when travelling, we recently encountered a corkscrew tethered to a bicycle-style metal security chain atop the minibar in a very upscale hotel room. *(See the gory visuals at* www.micahsolomon .com.*)* Make sure you're not similarly insinuating that your customers aren't trustworthy. If you are, it'll be hard to ask for *their* trust and loyalty in return.

Show, Don't Tell (And Don't Ever Just Point)

Don't give customers verbal directions. Getting directions in words is confusing and hard to remember. It unsettles people. When a customer asks how to get somewhere, physically lead him there.

The private jet-setters who stay in Leonardo's ultraluxury Capella resorts require a restroom as often as the rest of us. So, says Leonardo, "We don't tell them 'Go down the hall, turn right, walk fifteen feet, and then turn left.' We walk with them until the last turn. Then we back away, for discretion." Or, as the Capella service standard spells it out: "Escort guests until they feel comfortable with the directions or make visual contact with their destination."

This dictum has spread to other top service establishments. According to Phoebe Damrosch, formerly of Thomas Keller's four-star restaurant *Per Se,* Rule #20 in Keller's guidelines is "When asked, guide guests to the bathroom instead of pointing." (Phoebe also mentions a side effect we ourselves haven't experienced: Some of the male diners, she says, seemed confused, perhaps mistakenly thinking that she planned to accompany them in and help. "The eighteen percent you will leave me, sir, I always wanted to say, would not cover that."[3])

Phone and Internet Language and Communication Pointers

➤ **Here's our advice about screening your calls:** ***Don't do it.*** Just don't! And do your best not to have anybody, anywhere in your business, screen calls.

This is perhaps our most wildly unpopular idea. When clients first hear it, they usually tell us we're crazy. (You hate it too, right?) But our experience demonstrates that this single change can greatly enhance customer satisfaction—and as a fringe benefit, organizational effectiveness.

What's wrong with screening? There is no faster way to alienate potential customers (and business allies) than to make them run a gauntlet before you'll speak with them. If someone wants to talk with you, *let him*. If you're not the right person, you can quickly and politely transfer his call onward. How well this works will astound you.

What if you *do* need to screen your calls? (Maybe you're CEO Jeff Bezos at Amazon.com, and potential vendors won't give you a moment's peace, even though you're the wrong person for them to speak with.) At least create a discreet call-screening protocol that protects the feelings of callers:

> **Bad Screen:** "Who's calling?" (Whether or not this is followed by a grudging "please.") "Does he know why you are calling?" "Who are you with?" "What is the nature and purpose of your call?"
> **Good Screen:** "Absolutely. May I tell Mr. Bezos who is calling?" (In reality, the caller won't necessarily get Jeff. But hackles aren't raised; feelings are spared. There's no feeling of a test that must be passed—even if, in fact, there is.)

We, by the way, put our mouths where our mouths are, so to speak. Leonardo and Micah—as well as the best bosses we've had in our own careers—are non-phone-screeners. And historically, many titans of industry, up to and including Sam Walton, have been famously accessible on the phone. (We do figure Sam did a few backflips in his grave when Walmart announced years later that online customers were to be banned from even basic 800 telephone support as part of an official Walmart "Customer Contact Reduction" program.)[4]

➤ **To "give good phone," you've got to pick it up!** While you're busy getting your words just right, you also need to set the stage correctly. Answer the phone in the right number of rings: One or two rings is best, and try to never wait more than three rings.

Here's why: After three rings, which is roughly twelve seconds, callers become anxious. After five or six rings, they become frustrated. After eight or nine, quite irritated. After eleven or twelve, they will of course become angry or alarmed, and will hang up. Explain these reasons to your staff, and they will be more apt to support the no-more-than-three-rings policy because they'll understand how much it reduces client anxiety.

In cyberspace, there are analogs to answering your phone promptly. The following may sound obvious, but bear with us, because we see ugly surprises in this area all the time. Do you know for sure that the "request for info" forms on your website actually get where they're going once a customer fills them out? And, if so, whether they're answered quickly? You may be surprised to learn that because of a scripting error they never end up anywhere. Or, almost as bad, that they are delayed at some point in your processes and responded to *en masse* days later—which is a completely unacceptable interval on the Web. These service failures are invisible at the time, but they will ultimately show up in the form of stalled company growth.

Your technical team can help with elaborate and "statistically valid" testing systems to prevent these problems, which is very important. But please *supplement* these with a simple reality check any time you get that unsettled feeling inside: Try everything out yourself, as if you were a prospect or a customer. Do this repeatedly, and take nothing for granted. This "trust no one" technique puts you in the tiny minority who actually know that their systems work from their customers' perspective.

➤ **On the Internet, nobody knows you're human (so go out of your way to prove it).** Many businesses use Internet tricks as a way to give themselves a phony patina of personalization. As a result, even live customer service staffers attempting to engage online customers one on one may be met with inordinate suspicion. There are ways to turn these negative expectations to your advantage—by flipping them on their heads in a very visible manner. Here are a few examples:

> **If you send out any mass electronic messages, build in a way for customers to immediately reach a real person.** If you are one of the 60,000 people who has asked to receive an automated business email "from Micah Solomon" each month, try *responding* to one of the messages. Who gets right back to you? The *real* Micah. (See the sidebar for Micah's explanation of how he can do this and still get his other work done each day.) Compare this to the many online merchants whose mass email communications begin or end with something like:

"Please do not reply to this message."

To customers, that sounds a lot like:

"Hush now, customer: Don't distract us while we we're busy counting the money you paid us!"

It doesn't matter how competent, efficient, or technically "correct" your correspondence system is; if it makes you seem cold or robotic, your relationship with the customer will falter.

> **If your website features "live chat," make it clear you're staffing it with very real and personable human beings.** Even if you've manned Web chat lines with your very best, most expert staffers, users will devalue the service if you withhold full names. Not even your most personable, endearing employee is going to build enduring bonds for you online by typing, "Hi! This is Jane at Company X." Web visitors will assume that "Jane" is a corporate drone—or even a computer program!—sending canned advice out to customers she/it has no interest in hearing from again. This skepticism isn't *your* Jane's fault. It's the fault of all the artificial Janes before her. But it's easily remedied by calling her who she is: *Jane Chang-Katzenberg*.

> **Before anybody hits "send," make sure each email starts out on the right foot.** You would never begin a printed letter without some kind of salutation ("Dear," "Hi," etc.). So don't forget the salutation in an email. Even "Yo Mark!" (depending on the formality of your business and relationship, obviously) is better than starting cold with

just a name ("Mark—"), we'd argue. Try out this simple rule, and you'll start to feel your Internet relationships warm up.

Adding a Real Human Touch to a Mass Email Takes Less Time Than You'd Think

With a customer email list of 60,000, can you really find the time to answer replies from anyone who asks for you personally? Micah does so. He finds it less daunting than it sounds, and suggests you try it too. He explains:

"Most customers who've asked to receive a monthly informational or sales email from me don't actually feel a need to communicate one on one with me. So, if they respond it's by clicking on the automated link they were intended to click on (for whatever this month's offer is, for example). If someone's aggravated with our service, however, or someone wants to pitch his kid's Little League jersey sponsorship to me, I feel they ought to be able to get directly to me, right away, without going through any hoops. Because hopefully I can make sure we take care of the problem, or find someone who can, pronto. That's why I make sure that hitting "reply" or clicking on the "Micah" link sends a message directly to me.

"That's not very much to ask of my time. Only a few people use the option, and it's not difficult to set up—no matter what your Internet provider is telling you."

CHAPTER FOUR

Recovery!

Turning Service Failures Around

Breakdowns in service are unavoidable. An ice storm forces you to miss a customer's shipping deadline. A waiter drops a tray in a customer's lap. A computer system goes down. A key person walks out on you with no notice—on the only day you couldn't possibly arrange coverage.

All of this, potentially, is good news.

Service breakdowns are uncomfortable, and they require training to resolve. But you'll find an opportunity hidden inside your company's worst moments: the opportunity to bring a customer closer to you. Indeed, you can learn to handle service breakdowns so masterfully that they actually help you to create loyal customers. Our method is outlined below.

The Italian Mama Method

The archetype of an adoring Italian mother is the spirit behind our approach to service recovery. Picture a doting parent after a toddler takes a tumble:

> Oh, my darling, look at what happened! Oh, you skinned your knee on that walkway, my bambino; let me kiss that terrible wound. Shall we watch a little TV? And here's a lollipop for you while I bandage you up!

Minus the baby talk, this is pretty much how we recommend you react to service failures.

Does this style of response feel unfamiliar? That's understandable, since most service encounters seem to be based instead on what you might call the Courtroom Method:

> Let's sort out the facts of the situation. What was the angle of the concrete in the sidewalk at time of impact, and were you wearing proper protective clothing per the user's manual at the time your knee impacted the concrete? And I need to ask, young man: Were you exceeding the sidewalk speed limit?

The Four Steps to Great Service Recoveries

Reacting like trial lawyers is a hard habit for service providers to break. To get your staff out of the courtroom rut and ensure they don't lapse back into it, respond to each service failure with a specific stepwise sequence:

1. Apologize and ask for forgiveness.
2. Review the complaint with your customer.
3. Fix the problem and then follow up: Either fix the issue in the next twenty minutes or follow up within twenty minutes to check on the customer and explain the progress you have made. Follow up *after* fixing things as well, to show continuing concern and appreciation.

4. Document the problem in detail to allow you to permanently fix the defect by identifying trends.

Let's run through these steps in detail.

Step 1: Apologize and Ask for Forgiveness. What's needed is a sincere, personal, non-mechanical apology. There are many creative and sensitive ways to convey that you recognize and regret what your customer has been through.

What does a customer want out of an apology? He wants to be listened to, closely. He wants to know you're genuinely sorry. He wants to know you think he's right, at least in *some* sense. He wants to know you are taking his input seriously.

Overall, he wants to feel important to you.

This means that the key to an effective apology, to getting back on the right foot with your customer, is to convey at the outset that you are going to take his side and share his viewpoint.

Preemptively Unwad Your Staff's Shorts

When your own employees first hear you taking the customer's side, don't expect them to be thrilled. ("Does my boss blame me? Does she actually believe that idiot's version of what happened?") You need to explain that it's often necessary to empathize with and even amplify the customer's side of the story. Explain that the customer may or may not be right in an objective sense. Regardless, you're going to be disproportionately sympathetic to the customer's viewpoint because the customer is *your* boss—the customer pays *your* paycheck, along with the paychecks of everyone else in the company.

Human nature being what it is, this explanation will bear repeating. Often.

Pay close attention to *how* you apologize, because apologies that come off as insincere will alienate customers. If you're like the rest of us, you'll sometimes feel an urge to earnestly *pretend* you're apologizing, when you're in fact mounting a canny defense argument. Learn to sniff out fake apologies—your own and your staff's—in order to protect your relationships with customers.

Fake apologies can be very sneaky. Some don't reveal themselves as fakes until you have time to think them through carefully. For example, consider the apparently simple sentence "Please accept my apology." If that sentence is offered in a rushed, impersonal manner, it will come across as an order: *"Accept my apology already so we can wrap this up. We need to move on here!"*

Here is another great example of a sneaky fake apology: *"If what you say is correct, I certainly apologize."* (Translation: You, dear customer, are a liar.)

This one doesn't count, either: *"I'm sorry to hear that. We have wonderful receptionists. So I'm surprised to hear that you're unhappy."* (Translation: *"If you can't get along with* her, *you can't get along with anyone."*)

One key to an effective apology is to *stretch the apology out,* extending it until the customer begins to really connect with you. Stretching out an apology feels awkward at first, and it's hard for staff to do. In part this is because service providers tend to be action-oriented: They naturally want to dive in and fix things right away. It's good to be practical, of course, but service recovery is not just a no-nonsense, nuts-and-bolts process. Service recovery is an emotional and personal moment in a relationship. To connect with customers emotionally, slow apologies down.

Slowing down apologies gets easier with practice, and the technique's payoff is worth the investment: Gradually, the customer's anger will start to give way to goodwill. When an unrushed apology has finally defused a customer's anger, she will spontaneously signal that she is beginning to feel allied with you by saying something like "I understand that it's not personally your fault." This improvement in tone tells you that you're ready for Step 2.

Step 2: Go Over the Complaint with Your Customer. In Step 1, you've begun an alliance with your customer; in Step 2, those collaborative feelings will let you explore what she needs for a good outcome.

Fully exploring the customer's issue often requires you to ask rudimentary questions—even ones that can feel insulting to a customer, like "Are you sure you typed your password correctly?" We refer to these as DYPII ("Did You Plug It In?") questions. DYPII questions are likely to get customer hackles up. If you raise DYPII questions *before* you've finished Step 1, they'll often be considered offensive. But *after* you've developed collaborative feelings in Step 1, the same questions are generally tolerated well.

Just hold off with all the DYPIIness for now. Don't leap straight into problem solving.

You and your customer will get there eventually, together.

The Language of Service Recovery

Language, as mentioned in Chapter 3, is crucial in service recovery and needs to be addressed in a lexicon you create for your business. Little matters more when making a recovery: You'll never successfully get through it without the right words and phrasing. "I'm sorry, I apologize" are the words, delivered sincerely, that your customer wants to hear. Phrases like "It's our policy" and any synonyms for "You're wrong" must be banished.

If, in fact, the customer is wrong and there is a bona fide (e.g., safety-related or legally required) reason to point this out, you need words that express this obliquely—such as "Our records seem to indicate" and "Perhaps_____" so that she can realize her error but also save face.

In fact, the classically infuriating DYPII question, "Did you plug it in?" can be rendered as *"Maybe the wall connection is loose. Can you do me a favor and check where it plugs into the socket?"*

Step 3: Fix the Problem and Then Follow Up. So you've decided to re-place a substandard service or product. That's a step in the right direc-tion—but it's only a first step. Remember that the customer has been stressed, inconvenienced, and slowed down by your company. Merely giving her back what she expected to receive is not going to restore satisfaction.

A key principle in fixing a problem is to resolve the customer's sense of injustice—of having been wronged or let down. You do this by providing something *extra*.

You can find a way to restore the smile to almost any customer's face, whether it's a free upgrade or a more creative offering, like one-on-one consultation time with an expert on your staff. Collaborate with your wronged customer to figure out what would feel like valuable compensation to her, or use your initiative to get going in the right direction.

Ideally, your "something extra" will change the nature of the event for her: your special and creative efforts on her behalf will come to the foreground in the picture of the event she paints for herself and others, online or off, and the initial problem will move to the background.

For some customers the most valuable compensation isn't *material*. Some customers respond most positively to a chance to help improve your company. These customers want most of all to help make your service better, protect future customers from any similar wrongs, or feel assured that their advice is important to you. More often than not they do have insightful ideas about how to improve your business. So when a customer even hints at this motive, listen particularly closely and ap-preciatively to the suggestions you receive and make it clear that you will be passing the ideas along.

Customers who express critiques or suggestions are often expressing a desire to be involved in your company. In a way, they are offering themselves as unpaid volunteers. This sense of connection goes a long way toward helping them to become loyal to you. Don't squander the opportunity to connect with them during a service failure.

The Elements of Follow-Up

Various approaches to the follow-up are appropriate in different service settings, but they all should include *immediate, internal,* and *wrap-up* components. Together, the goal of these components is to ensure that the recovery goes correctly, that your customer feels appropriately taken care of, and that your organization gets the full benefit of customer loyalty from your recovery efforts.

Immediate Follow-Up If you've handled the problem yourself, check in promptly with the customer after the intended resolution. This underscores your concern. It also lets you catch lingering unresolved issues. Immediate follow-up is also important when you have *reassigned* the customer's problem to somebody else. For example: Suppose that you work in sales. A customer calls you (because you're the person she knows) to report being inconvenienced by a glitch on your website. Naturally, you hand off the technical resolution of the problem to your IT department. But will you ever know if IT actually ends up implementing a workable solution for your customer? Whether she ends up feeling taken care of by the technician? *You'll only find out if you check back in.* Customers want *you,* their original ally, to follow up on such questions, not just somebody over in IT, not even if you know for a fact that the IT person is best equipped to help.

Internal Follow-up Others in your organization need to be alerted *immediately* to the service failure a customer experienced. Here's why such service failure alerts are a hallmark of exceptional businesses:

➤ Your staff will know that any further interactions with this customer should be rechecked *beyond* the usual quality control.

➤ Your staff is cued to interact with the customer appropriately after the failure. It is not the customer's responsibility to explain his troubles once again—unless he wants to. Nor should he be forced to "act happy" to match your staff's incorrect expectations. They should already be aware of what he's been through. For example: A restaurant can grace the departures of such customers with relevant words of thanks from the manager or maitre d': "Your business means a lot to us, and we appreciate your patience this evening: I'm so sorry about the mix-up with your entrées and look forward to doing a better job for you next time." That beats an off-puttingly cheery "How was everything this evening?" that makes it sound like the left hand doesn't know that the right hand dropped the soufflé.)

> You can flag the unfortunate customer's file for special treatment during her next visit or transaction—even if that special treatment is just the ability to return a knowing look or to share a laugh at your own expense.

Wrap-Up: Solidify your relationship with the customer by following up again with a handwritten note or phone call when the episode is over: "I'm sorry you experienced this problem. I'm so pleased to have you as a customer, and I am looking forward to welcoming you back." Doing this by email is all right if you're solely an online business, but it won't have the same impact.

Step 4: Document the Problem in Detail. It's natural to want to give yourself a breather after solving a customer's problem. Still, make sure your staff is trained to record, every single time, the details of what went wrong—promptly, before the memory can fade or distort. We call this the *deposition.* Be scrupulous: The only way to prevent serious problems from recurring is to document the problem for careful analysis later.

Depending on your business, depositions can be high-tech or low-tech. The information can initially go into an incidents box, a problem log, or a verbal report, or it can be entered directly into its final software destination. In all cases, the documentation should include fairly detailed information. The particular details will depend on your business, but they usually include such notes as the time of day, the type of product or service, how busy your business was at the time, and the details of the customer's circumstances.

Your goal in using this documentation is to identify trends or patterns that hint at underlying causes. For example, you might notice that a problem tends to happen around 3:30 p.m. on Wednesdays when Billy is on the job. This could lead you to consider whether Billy may have missed a particular training module. Or it happens only between 8:30 and 9:30 a.m., which leads you to notice that a freight elevator is always under maintenance at that time, creating unacceptably slow service. Or the complaints are always about rear wiper blades you sell, but only in your Eastern and Midwest franchises, leading you to discover an interaction between salted roads and the particular rear blades you stock. Or the complaints occur only when you are above 90 percent of your customer capacity, leading you to study whether your business can learn to run effectively at 90 percent-plus capacity (as a Disney theme park can manage to do), or if you need to build additional capacity or limit your clientele.

How Should You Compensate a Customer for a Service or Product Failure?

It depends. And that variability, in fact, is what's most important. Customers have diverse values and preferences—so your people who placate disgruntled customers need to be given enormous discretion. Still, there are principles that apply:

➤ *Most customers understand that things can and will go wrong.* What they do not understand, accept, or find interesting are excuses. For example, they don't care about your org chart: Your mentioning that a problem originated in a different department is of no interest to them.

➤ *Don't panic.* Customers' sense of trust and camaraderie *increases* after a problem is successfully resolved, compared to if you had never had the problem in the first place. This makes sense, since you now have a shared experience: You have solved something by working closely together.

➤ *Avoid assuming you know what solution a customer wants or "should" want.* Ask. And if a customer makes a request that sounds extreme or absurd, don't rush to dismiss it. Even if it seems on its face impossible, there may be a creative way to make the requested solution, or something a lot like it, happen.

➤ *Don't strive for "fairness" or "justice."* Our archetypal doting Italian mama doesn't investigate whether her bambino obeyed the sidewalk speed limit before comforting him, and a customer's warm feelings for a company aren't about fairness. They're about being treated especially well.

➤ *Learn from customer issues, but don't use them as an opportunity to discipline or train your staff* in front of *your customer.* This may sound obvious, but it happens quite often. Watch out for this flaw, especially when you're under stress.

➤ *Don't imagine you're doing something special for a customer by making things how they should have been in the first place.* Time cannot be given back—it's gone. The chance to get it right the first time? It's gone. So re-creating how things should have been is just a first step. You need to then give the customer something extra. Mama bandages a knee *and* offers a lollipop. If you aren't sure which "extra" to offer a particular customer, just make it clear you want to offer something. If the customer doesn't like red lollipops or doesn't eat sugar, she'll let you know. Then you can decide together on a different treat.

➤ *Keep in mind the lifetime value of a loyal customer.* A loyal customer is likely worth a small fortune to your company when considered over a decade or two of regular purchases. We have done lifetime customer value studies in our own companies and client companies, and frequently found the lifetime value of a loyal customer to be *up to $100,000*—and occasionally even more. Perhaps in your business this number is a few thousand

dollars, or possibly it is half a million. It is well worth figuring out
that number and keeping it in mind if you ever feel that temptation to quarrel with a customer over, say, an overnight shipping
bill.

Use Your Own Experience to Prepare You

Disastrous handling of service breakdowns assault us everywhere in our
daily lives. Our suggestion: Begin to use the world as your private research laboratory. Whenever poor problem resolution intrudes on you
as a consumer, think about what was done wrong and how you as a
provider could have resolved the failure better. That way, you're less
likely to go ballistic from all the abuses you suffer as a consumer. (Hey,
now you're *using* your frustrating experiences for your own company's
benefit.)

Here's an example from Leonardo's daily life. A few years ago, he
decided to redo his basement. Like other parents before him, he felt
safer imagining his kids entertaining their friends at home where he
could keep tabs on them. He decided to really do things up in a big
way:

> So I ask my two boys, "What would you like in the basement?"
> "I want a foosball." Easy enough.
> "I want a basketball court." Not so easy, that one.
> Both boys agree they want a big-screen TV. Doting father that I am, I
> go to one of those stores and buy a big-screen TV. The price, to be honest,
> was a shocker. And what a beast to lug home.
> Now, while everyone else sees my warts life-size, my kids are still at
> an age where they see me a bit like a medieval knight with a beautiful horse
> and shining armor with the feathers and the sword and the cape.
> So I—I mean Sir Leonardo—and my boys take the TV out of the
> box. We're all excited. I plug it in. Nothing happens. Ding: the first ding
> in my armor.

"Daddy, what's wrong? What's wrong with the TV?"

I say: "I don't know. The TV's not working."

"You mean you don't know how to make it work?"

"Son, I know exactly how to make it work, but this thing is not working. Go check the breakers in the meantime."

My son checks the breakers. "They're fine."

I double-check the breakers. Yep, fine.

I fiddle with the plug, move the plug, move the TV. Nothing. Ding. Another ding in my armor.

Finally, I, uh, Sir Shrunkalot, concede defeat: We need to bring the TV back.

What a nuisance! Put the TV back in the box, load it into the car, drive to the store. Go to the customer service desk. I don't know why electronics stores do this, but they often put their most unfriendly, grudging people at the customer service desk. This one is no exception.

I say to this surly man, "Good afternoon, I just bought this TV and it doesn't work."

The man turns reluctantly away from some paperwork, looks at me, and says, slowly, "Well . . . did you plug it in?"

"Plug it in?" I ask with mock innocence. "What do you mean by that?" Customer service clerk: "You know . . . the plug goes in the wall . . . did you plug it in?" At this point, I admit, I get belligerent: "No . . . I just arrived from the depths of the untamed jungle last week. What is this concept called 'plugging in?' I thought this thing would spirit itself to life!" (Pause . . . the clerk is considering his next move—which might be to call security.) "Of course I plugged it in. What kind of question is that!?"

At length, he checks the TV. No life. After this development, he's suddenly full of flowery sentences, but they only concern how wonderful and reliable this brand of TV has always been. Nothing about my predicament. I was honestly starting to think I had made a mistake (had the boys and I in fact plugged it in?). Finally, he replaces the TV. Before putting it in the car, I say, "Now you plug it in and see if it works." The thing works; I take it home.

So they restored the original product. But am I happy with the process? Am I satisfied? Of course not."

This example illustrates how service recovery fails when you don't follow the principles and steps we outline in this chapter. Think of what is going awry here:

First, did the right staff member deliver the service? An employee in a position like this should have strong empathy, as well as problem-solving ability. The employee Leonardo encountered lacked both.

Were the steps delivered in order? The DYPII question—literally "Did You Plug It In?" in this case—was asked too early. It was asked before an apology was made, let alone accepted.

Did the employee make any attempt to discover Leonardo's needs? This service rep failed to understand and solve either Leonardo's most important loss—the dings in his parental armor—or his secondary losses: time, hassle, frustration, even wear and tear on his car upholstery. In other words, the service rep failed to figure out what the customer really needed to restore his satisfaction. The rep assumed that replacement of defective goods is enough to satisfy an inconvenienced customer.

It isn't.

What, if anything, *could* such a store have done to restore Sir Shrunkalot's shining armor? In fact, they could have satisfied him easily and cheaply.

For example, suppose that the service rep had said, with genuine concern and even a conspiratorial tone: "Sir, I'm terribly sorry. These are made for us overseas, and they are supposed to be spot-checked before they get in the store. I realize it's small comfort to know you ended up on the wrong end of a statistic, so if you make another purchase here in the future, please ask for me personally, and I'll check it out in the store with you before you schlep it home. Today, though, do you have a favorite DVD?"

Leonardo would have said, "Well, actually this TV is for my boys, and they've been dying to see the latest live concert video from Swirly Goo and the Goners."

The rep would have then replied, "Sir, may I go through the aisle with you, and see if I can help you find a 'Swirly' DVD your boys would want, to show our appreciation for your business and for your patience? We're really so sorry that this happened to them, and to you. I hope that you will forgive us and give us an opportunity to serve you well next time."

Leonardo would have taken the DVD and felt repaid in some small way for his trouble.

Think about this: What's the wholesale cost of that DVD? Seven dollars? By investing seven dollars in a customer who'd just spent more than a thousand dollars, what would the store accomplish? They would be taking a serious step toward winning a lifetime customer. Plus, imagine the improvement they'd be making in the story Leonardo and his family would tell if anyone asked about their new TV.

And as for Leonardo, he could have gone home to his kids, head held high, and said, "Hey, these TVs are all built overseas these days, and some of them don't quite work right after they've bounced around for days in the container ship. But I've got it all handled now."

Who Should Handle Customer Complaints?

Everyone should handle customer complaints. Of course, not everybody is going to be equally involved in customer service, nor should each employee be trained in the most specialized service. We do believe it is important that all employees participate to *some* degree—to the extent of their trainability and the extent to which they interact with customers.

But who should handle cases that can't be resolved by a staffer on the front lines? In other words, who should serve as "the manager" for a customer who demands to "speak with a manager"? Here are a couple of guidelines:

➤ Empower your employees to be able to resolve the issue whenever possible without getting to the "manager" level.

➤ When unavoidable, you need the designated "manager" to stand out in two areas: as a sharp and eager problem solver *and* as a virtuoso at connecting empathically with people. If you've hired and trained appropriately, all of your staff will have some strength in these areas. But only about one in ten will be unusually gifted in both areas. Those ten percent should be your designated service "managers"—if indeed you choose to have such a position.

What we're recommending here is that you avoid anything like an old-style isolated Complaints Department. Instead, teach your staff that Joan in Sales and Jeff in Shipping can themselves initiate a service recovery. Jeff may not be the right person to fix the problem, but if he encounters an unsatisfied customer, he must know how to say much more than "I can't help you, I just send boxes."

Even Dale, who cleans the toilets, should be empowered beyond helpless reactions like "*Um, you'd need to ask a manager about that.*" Customers hate to hear "You'll need to ask a manager."

Dale will feel better about himself and your company, his customer will feel better about herself and your company, and service problems will tend to turn out better if Dale has been trained to express confident enthusiasm: "*Certainly, I am so sorry. I will help you with that,*" followed by finding the right person to solve the problem—even if that does happen to be, in fact, a manager.

(Airlines provide a perplexing example here: Why *can't* you complain to the pilot about a customer service issue—assuming you're not midflight? Or to the ramp agent? The response should include, "*I'm terribly sorry about what happened*" followed by assistance getting you to the right person to get your issue fixed. *If you wear the uniform, you represent the company.*)

If you're going to involve the whole company in customer service, we recommend you involve them fully: entrust them with broad discretionary powers to respond flexibly, creatively, and intensively to service errors.

Probably the most famous example of total customer service empowerment is the carte blanche monetary discretion The Ritz-Carlton has given to staff members for decades: $2,000 per employee per customer, to be used to solve any customer complaint in the manner the employee felt was appropriate. How could so much creative and monetary freedom succeed? It works like this: If you start off defensive, rigid, or withholding, people tend to respond by escalating their demands. It's a classic vicious cycle. But if you can start from an accepting, flexible, and generous position, people naturally feel inclined to be reasonable in return. The cycle turns virtuous. Indeed, Horst Schulze, who initiated this policy in the 1980s (when, although it's hard to fathom now, $2,000 would buy more than a dozen nights at the fanciest Ritz), and Leonardo, who has been involved in continuing and expanding it with Horst at The Ritz-Carlton, Capella, and Solis hotels, verify that an employee has *never* had to resort to using all of that discretion. Still, knowing it is there has been a great builder of strength and responsibility for employees. Think about its value as an ongoing training tool: It serves as a reminder of management's belief in honoring a guest's potential lifetime value—and is proof that management is willing to put money behind that belief.

So in order to keep customers happy, your people will need to be able to respond in an empowered and immediate way to service failures—without waiting for a manager's okay. This carte blanche approach has grown even more important in these days of customer rebellions Twittering out of control: Only with immediate and broad discretionary powers is there a chance your frontline employees will be able to defuse complaints *before* they get posted online.

Subtle Is Beautiful: Service Recovery Below the Radar

The most beautiful service failure recoveries can be so small and subtle that a customer won't notice the failure, only the intimacy the recovery brings.

We enjoy, as much as anyone, the grand, broad-stroke stories that are popular in customer service lore, like the famous story of Nordstrom accepting defective tires as a customer return—even though Nordstrom doesn't sell tires. These stories are great for training and great for spreading a company's reputation. But, we also admire service professionals who can discern *small* failures in systems and similarly small dissatisfactions in failed customer interactions—and compensate effectively so the customer can get right back on track.

Last fall, Micah noticed a saleswoman looking for fresh *New York Times* subscribers at a crafts fair in the Pennsylvania countryside. She had brought along some high-quality *New York Times* gift items as incentives and she gave her pitch as people passed:

Sales Rep: *"Subscribe to New York Times home delivery, only $X a week. Get great gifts!"*

Micah: "Sorry. Already subscribe."

Sales Rep: *"Are you getting all seven days delivered currently? I can upgrade you if you aren't."*

Micah (chuckling at her persistence): "Unless you're going to start a new evening edition, I don't think there's a way we can get more papers delivered than we already do."

Sales Rep: *"But these are nice gifts, aren't they? I'm going to give you something anyway, for being a great customer. What would you like?"*

Let's look at this encounter. First, some overall observations. Note that Micah was just walking by at a crowded crafts fair. He hadn't asked the *Times* rep for anything and hadn't offered her anything in terms of making her numbers. He also hadn't said anything about wanting the gifts. She could, however, sense the imbalance in the encounter, having nothing to offer one of the paper's "full fare" passengers.

So she decided to extend exceptional, anticipatory service to someone who wasn't even the target customer of the promotion.

Now, let's examine the individual elements of this encounter.

Was there a service failure here? Yes, a very small one. The *New*

York Times, like many companies, was running a spiffy promotion intended to grab *new* customers. Super. But studies show that *existing* customers are the ones who pay the most attention to everything you do as a brand. The *Times* didn't have a plan for how to treat existing customers who might respond to their representatives' overtures. This created a socially awkward moment for their loyal customers who were walking by the sales stand: "I'm a loyal customer, but you can't sign me up, and so we have nothing more to say to each other."

Perhaps this service deficiency was foreseeable. But you can't foresee every shortfall in your business. Every situation, and every customer, is different.

This is why you need aware, appropriately trained people. The *Times'* sales rep was savvy and empathic enough to notice a service deficiency, even though it was only implicit.

In your organization, when an employee comes back to the office after an episode like this, is she praised for recognizing an issue and supporting an existing customer, who is arguably more important than an impulsive new one? Or is her hand slapped because she came back to the office one gift short? Would she get bragging rights if you noticed her profiled in this chapter, or would you worry that you really couldn't afford to have your employees improvising in this manner?

More generally: Do you hire the appropriate people, give them the discretionary power they need, and praise them when they fill in the gaps in your systems, thereby catching customers before they fall out? We hope by the end of this book you will be answering "yes" to all of the above.

Write-Offs Lead to Write-Offs

It doesn't always feel good to go to extreme lengths to pacify a customer. It can be hard to remember the upside, to know that your work is ultimately going to pay off. So here's an overriding philosophy which can help you through thankless moments: *Individual customers are irreplaceable.* Regardless of the size of your market segment, once you start writing off customers, we can predict the day in the future when you'll be out of business. (We'll chart it on a big piece of paper for you if you like.) Think you have a huge market and it's okay to kiss off customers and replace them down the road? We all watched Detroit automakers make that assumption and let imports chip away at the edges until there was little remaining as a core.

We suggest in the strongest terms that you think of every one of your customers as a core customer—and treat the loss of a customer as a tragedy to be avoided.

CHAPTER FIVE

Keeping Track to Bring Them Back

Tracking Customer Roles, Goals, and Preferences

Even if you hired a platoon of statisticians to pore through your customer data, they'd never uncover a single style of "good service" that can please every customer. Good service requires custom fitting. This is one principle on which true customer service virtuosos—successful barkeeps, booksellers, shopkeepers, and maitre d's—agree.

So, to succeed far beyond a Mom and Pop scale, or even to run a Mom and Pop that continues to thrive when Mom and Pop are chillin' in Cancun, you need to ensure that all of your employees are able to provide individualized service—no matter how briefly they've been part of your team and no matter how poor their memories are.

The solution is to develop a tracking system that captures each customer's likes and dislikes, as well as what each customer personally values and is hoping for when doing business with you. After each customer interaction, your staff will use this system to *note* the idiosyncratic personal values and preferences of the customer and then *share* that information, however or wherever it is helpful within your company.

A commitment to systematic noting and sharing will separate you from that wonderful dry-cleaning business on the corner (the one that lost most of its customers when the owner fell ill). It will allow you to avoid the fate of the popular, lively restaurant in LA that never quite succeeded when it tried to open other locations.

Principles of Noting and Sharing

What follow are our key principles for building a successful system for the notation and sharing within your company of customer information.

Principle 1: Keep Your Systems Simple. Don't track too much stuff, and keep what you *do* track right at the fingertips of your frontline staff. Simplicity is what makes a preference-tracking system sustainable. If you obsessively gather gobs of data on every customer for hypothetical purposes, you're going to obscure the preferences you need ready access to. You'll also dilute the energy of your staff, who will lose track of the original goal: relating warmly to customers as individuals and making them feel important. This "Keep-Your-Systems-Simple" (KYSS) approach is almost always the best one, even in very complex customer contexts.

Setting Up the Ritz

Years ago, to begin building the customer service systems at The Ritz-Carlton, the staff were given notepads to write down guest preferences and concerns that they noticed or were alerted to. A guest who had recently sobered up wanted the mini-bar emptied prior to his arrival. One very allergic woman felt comfortable in her room only if she had ten boxes of tissues placed there. If housekeeping noticed that a solo guest turned down his bed on the left or on the right, this would be duly noted as the side to turn down in the evening. These were requests staff at The Ritz-

Carlton wanted to honor on each subsequent visit *without* being asked—in whichever Ritz properties throughout the world these guests next visited.

In their initial, groundbreaking system, the Ritz-Carlton team gave themselves the goal of notating just five preferences—and then satisfying at least three of them. The result was a *transformative* impact on the guest experience, as has been well documented in the business press, for example in this traveler interview by Gary Heil and his co-authors from their book *One Size Fits One*:

> *The hypoallergenic pillows we requested during our last stay are on the bed, all fluffed up—and we forgot to ask this time. There are numerous extra towels (and we remember we had called room service for extras during our last visit). The cookies on the tray are all chocolate chip, our favorite kind—and the oatmeal ones we received last time but didn't eat are mysteriously missing. When we checked in, the concierge asked us if we wanted tickets to the symphony as we had requested last time.*
>
> *We begin to realize that The Ritz-Carlton has taken every bit of information it learned about us from our last visit and indexed it in a database. Before our arrival, the hotel staff, from room service staff to the chambermaid, customized our room with the extra touches they knew we would want or need. They seem to know us as individuals and they seem to care genuinely whether our stay is enjoyable.[1]*

The impetus for the Ritz's simple tracking system, Leonardo explains, came from an early finding: "We're always asking customers for their expectations and desires from our properties. The most common answer we heard—and even to this day hear—is *'We want it to be like home.'* But when we probed guests for the unexpressed need beneath this not-quite-convincing answer, it turns out it's not *their* home they want. It's the dream of a childhood home that they're looking for—you know, the home where everything is taken care of for you."

At home as a typical adult, you are in control, but only on a self-serve basis. In your childhood home (optimally), it was a different sort of experience. Food appeared at mealtimes. You didn't have to worry about shopping for personal items. When light bulbs blew out, new ones replaced them. When you left, your parents were genuinely saddened by your departure, and they looked forward to seeing you again. Most of all, your personal preferences in all of these matters were well known and "magically" taken into consideration.

Once the Ritz-Carlton management team recognized that this was what their customers were seeking, they were able to develop a better and more customized service model. In Leonardo's newest hotel brands, in fact, they are extending this concept by pre-interviewing guests to see if they can help reduce uncertainties that *precede* the customer's arrival—transportation and other logistical issues, for instance—to ensure they feel cared for from the moment they arrive in the city. A bit like Mom might do if she knew you were on your way back to town.

Principle 2: If It's Important to Your Customer, It Belongs in Your System. In the independent music and film industries where his company operates, Micah makes a point of using software to allow his staff to capture information in specific categories, such as which genre of music and instrument a customer plays, as well as unique details of nearly any sort in which the customer shows interest or appears to take pride in. This latter, general category may include a big movie the client has worked on, a treasured industry award he has received, and so on. Or, it might be more important to use this space to note that his wife is ill and that he hates being called on the phone in the morning. We call these data points *Roles, Goals, and Preferences.*

Even in the tiniest of companies, roles, goals, and preferences should be tracked consistently. When Micah first started his business ventures, his "empire" consisted entirely of himself taking phone orders and processing them—in the leaky basement of a starter home. Micah could have personally stayed on top of the roles, goals, and preferences of each of his (few!) early customers. But after hearing the first employee he hired struggle to chat with a big musical client ("Who's your drummer again?"), he became an early advocate and developer of automated systems to track roles, goals, and preferences. Without these systems, his employees wouldn't have been able to deliver the "Mom's house" experience as his company grew.

Startups often use off-the-shelf software to manage customer preferences. Be careful: Some such programs do not carry forward notations from individual project records into the customer's permanent record. Leaving a customer's preferences languishing as notations in a single project's record is no better than a scribble in a restaurant's reservation book. (That "classic" method means that unless the restaurant goes through all the reservations ever made, it's going to miss the 2005 entry where the gent now being seated mentioned his shellfish allergy.) Put durable information about each customer in that customer's *permanent* database record. And make sure that preference data is easily visible from within any project he does with you moving forward.

What types of items should go in your tracking system? Track whatever is most important to the customer. Customers' roles, goals, and preferences are quite diverse, and no amount of market research can predict them perfectly. Here are some items that we recommend you keep at your fingertips:

➤ **Information on any missteps on past projects/visits/transactions with a particular customer.**

➤ **Information on any problems that have already occurred on this visit, or that seem to be unfolding at that moment.** As we have already discussed, a customer who has already received poor service on this visit shouldn't, later on in the visit, receive oblivious, chirpy greetings from other staff members ("Are you enjoying your time with us so far?"), requiring the customer to educate the staff over and over ("Actually, it's been problematic") in response.

> **Product/service preferences, whether stated by the customer or observed, which you should try to accommodate without being asked.**

> **Anything your customer filled out earlier on a comment card or electronic survey.** These forms contain not just statistical data but feelings expressed by a real, live customer. In addition to responding to such feedback personally and promptly (see Chapter 6), include this information in the customer's tracking file so that you can keep it in mind when working with the customer in the future.

> **Any personal ties to your establishment, such as a shared history, friends the customer has who work at your establishment, etc.** Some of your customers will perceive your business in especially emotional, personal terms. Encourage this. For example, if a customer explains that she first visited your drugstore with her dad as a child thirty years ago, be enthusiastic about that. Then write it down. As another example, some of your customers may express special attachment to a particularly charismatic member of your team. Record those feelings, and cue that employee to be sure to make contact with the customer. The employee's personal contact will enhance loyalty far more than a discount.

> **The number of projects/purchases/visits.** Make sure your tracking system identifies unusually valuable customers clearly.

> **Especially challenging customers.** Never write notes about challenging customers except in a tactful code. Any such warning must be reviewed by someone in an ownership position before being shared, even in your internal, password-protected computer system. Among the reasons for this caution: Many "intractably" difficult customers are actually misunderstood customers responding to a specific situation; the next time you encounter them they may be as easy as the day is long.

So while service establishments often do have codes that alert staff to troublesome customers, it's crucial to keep such negative notations secret, and only maintain them with the approval of senior staff. (Speaking more broadly, there is emotional value in reframing how you talk, and type, about customers. Using less judgmental language toward customers in your own notations and discussions will actually help soften your feelings. For example, try: *demanding* rather than *difficult*, *has discriminating tastes* in place of *impossible to please*, and even *very time-focused* instead of *impatient*.)

➤ **Personal facts: spouse, pets, kids, etc.** If included, such details need to be accurately dated. (For example: Pets noted five years ago are, sadly, not safe to inquire about. Husband you haven't heard mentioned in a few years? Probably ditto.) Use a software system that automatically time-stamps entries.

Privacy training and systems security are critical parts of any professional setup. And for added peace of mind, *assume* your files are a lot less private than you think. We consulted with one company that was still reeling from an IT initiative designed to allow customers direct account access. The initiative's goal had been to cut staffing costs by increasing customer self-service. Unfortunately, in the new system it was possible for customers to be inadvertently greeted online with their personal tracking files—which in one mortifying instance included very embarrassing comments, written in quite plain English! This kind of self-inflicted privacy breach is not uncommon. And demanding customers are particularly unforgiving. So figure out a useful code, swear all parties to secrecy, and stick to the code.

Principle 3: The Information You Gather Needs to be Available in Real Time. Years ago, Leonardo's team committed to making information about guests available throughout each location in an appropriate way that made guests feel good. Of course, the most basic guest information is the guest's name, which is noted carefully upon arrival, and then used—graciously and with correct pronunciation—throughout the property, a technique that truly feels like magic to customers. (Discreet radio communication plus an attentive staff makes this "magic trick" possible.) See if there are ways to adapt this magic to your own business in creative ways.

For example, perhaps you run a managed health care facility rather than a hotel. Most of us know from personal experience how unsettling it feels when a nurse comes through the doors into the waiting room and calls like an auctioneer to everybody in the room: "Julia Jones!?" Talk about starting off on the wrong foot with your customers! Considering the hidden benefits of positive word of mouth from satisfied and loyal customers—and the hidden costs of alienating such a customer— it's well worth finding a better way. (In health care fields, those hidden costs can be astronomical, due to the increased risk of a lawsuit from a dissatisfied patient.)

Once you're committed to treating your patients like royalty from your first words, how would you do it? You could begin by training your receptionists to write down each arriving patient's type of clothing or other politely identifiable features. (Julia Jones, 45, red blouse, blue slacks, blond.) These notes could then be carried along with the patient's medical paperwork to the nurse who leads the patients in. Armed with these notes, the nurse can then find Julia and give her a warm, personable welcome when she's ready to bring her back for treatment.

Principle 4: Preferences Change; Assumptions Are Tricky. Preference tracking can run amuck. One of our favorite chefs, Patrick O'Connell of The Inn at Little Washington, tells this story:

> Recently I stayed at a New York hotel that prides itself on customized service. The first morning, I had breakfast in the hotel restaurant, and I ordered tea. The next day, the waiter brought me tea as soon as I sat down. Unfortunately, that day I wanted coffee.[2]

Missteps like this shouldn't stop you from using your preference tracking system as a starting point. If that same restaurant had greeted Patrick with a cordial "Good morning, Mr. O'Connell. Will you be having tea again? Would you like it again today with the Turbinado sugar?" that could have been splendid. *(Note: Preferences we've ascribed to Chef O'Connell's taste buds are for illustrative purposes only.)*

Principle 5: Moods Change: Track Them. There is an additional human metric we encourage you to track: *changes in your customer's level of enjoyment over the course of your customer's interaction with you.* The Inn at Little Washington's O'Connell is the architect of one of the simpler and more effective customer happiness tracking systems we've experienced. At his Virginia countryside restaurant, each server discreetly notes the level of guest happiness at the beginning of a meal, rating it from 1 to 10. (So discreetly, in fact, that we never see them assessing us or logging their conclusions—no matter how often we conduct delicious "research" in Patrick's dining room.) The goal is to bring the mood of the guests up to at least 9 before they hit the road for the ride home. Of course, how you track this in your own business will depend on how long delivery takes for your particular product or service and how complex other demands are on your staff's attention.

Principle 6: Don't Blow It with a Wooden Delivery. Information you cull from tracking needs to be used naturally and in a way that seems effortlessness to customers. As an example, Dale Carnegie's insight that one's own name is "the sweetest sound" has been endlessly quoted. He's right, too—but *mispronounce* that name, and "the sweetest sound" goes sour. (Trust guys named Leonardo Inghilleri and Micah Solomon on this one.) By the same token, don't ruin a great thing by inserting a customer's name or other personal information into the interaction in an artificial, fill-in-the-blank manner.

Have you ever called a help desk and had the person answer, "Good morning, thank you for calling XYZ, how may I help you?" and as soon as you give your name it's inserted into everything, without emotion, without passion, clearly running through a script that appears on the screen? You feel like you could shout out that your house is on fire, and you'd get the exact same vocal response from this mechanized, allegedly personalized service. There's no point gathering customer information if you're going to use it in a canned, robotic fashion.

Principle 7: Using Technology to Ask for Information? It's a Fine Line between Clever and Creepy. *Beware the protective bubble.* Everyone has what we call a "protective bubble" around himself, to a greater or lesser extent. Teaching your staff to recognize this and probe only gently, retreating as cued, is one of the keys to attentive service that we will discuss in detail in Chapter 7. But in electronic interactions you lose the human failsafe of direct verbal and nonverbal feedback. And as customers well know, electronic databases have the power to track *everything* in a way humans never would.

People respond skeptically when asked to help populate Internet databases. It's not like when you request information face-to-face: Personally ask somebody where he was born, and there is a high chance he'll answer openly. At worst you'll get a "Why do you want to know?" and thus a chance to retract the question or explain the reason for it. But if you require potential customers to divulge information on your company website, you'll never know whether the requirement drove them away. You won't realize that they thought your electronic persona was rude or that they didn't trust the website version of you. Inexplicably, you simply won't get signups.

The simplest solution is to remove all potentially intrusive questions from your Internet forms. An alternative is to make those questions optional, and fully explain your reasons for asking. Even customer-centered companies sometimes violate this rule; they may then experience a loss of market share or a drop in customer quality that they are never able to trace back to its origin.

In the physical realm, but with the "help" of technology, one family-oriented chain of mall stores crossed this line in their eagerness to use automation, and they may not even have realized it. This company overall has a lot going for it: It serves parents and young children alike, offering a warm and welcoming experience, with great potential to bond with customers. That is, until the last moment—when they encounter an intrusive electronic procedure near the final checkout counter. The checkout kiosk was placarded thus, in huge kiddie-style lettering, the most recent time we visited the store:

Input your
•Name
•Address
•Email address
•Gender
and
•Date of birth
in our Kiddie Carousel system and sign up to receive special offers.

On every screen was cheery animation coaxing things along, complete with letters made out of colorful stars and buttons to simulate a child's handwriting:

When is your birthday, [name of child from previous screen]?
•Month?
•Day?
•Year?
Press the pink key after each entry!

(Note: Security experts call date of birth, name, and address the "holy trinity," which, in combination with the often-breached social security number, lead most commonly to identity theft and other privacy problems. All items in this holy trinity are asked for in the sequence of questions above—and they're being asked of customers who haven't graduated elementary school.)

The temptation to enter an entire birth date is driven home by photos of a family birthday celebration. A small "adult supervision recommended" disclaimer seemed to have been hastily placed on a card atop the monitor, but was obscured from where you would be most likely to read it. Regardless, disclaimers don't win back your customer's loyalty. If customers feel you're being sneaky, they'll run the other way.

Surprises Are Hazardous—Online and Off

Just because you *can* get information doesn't mean you *should* get it. And just because you've gotten information doesn't make all uses of it appropriate. People don't always like being surprised—even if the surprise shows them the impressiveness of your service systems. "Permission marketing" expert Seth Godin gives these examples.

> If your credit card company called you up and said, "We've been looking over your records and we see that you've been having an extramarital affair. We'd like to offer you a free coupon for VD testing . . . ," you'd freak out, and for good reason. If the local authorities start using what's on the corner surveillance cameras to sell you a new kind of commuter token, you'd be a little annoyed at that as well.[3]

Those are of course hypotheticals from Seth, but what about *this* real-life example from a friend of ours who was staying at a top hotel? She called the front desk to complain about a problem with the service. The front desk clerk fixed the problem but added a mistake of his own: Reading from the output of the electronically monitored minibar in her room, he told her, "I see you enjoy vodka. Would you enjoy one of our new vodkas with your dinner tonight as an apology?" The clerk thought he was being clever, but he came off as basically spying in his guest's bedroom—not something that's going to warm the cockles of a customer's heart.

Keep in mind that you are gathering information *to serve your customer.* Any other use is at best secondary. And because we are talking about electronic systems, always remember the limitations of working without physical or auditory feedback. Do not require information unless it is an absolutely necessary part of doing business. When you ask for it, ask politely, never using the information in a way that penetrates someone's protective bubble.

How to Track Customer Preferences on the Internet—Without Intruding

The Internet tempts us to gather too much information. It's so easy to ask customers questions in an automated online interface that the temptation to "pile 'em on" can be very strong. Here are some principles to help you minimize this temptation:

1. If you must gather any sensitive information, explain why it's necessary—clearly and fully.

2. Never require a date of birth unless you must screen underage users. Many people will either exit a website or falsify their birth date online if it is required of them. Pressuring customers to lie to you is the wrong way to begin a journey toward loyalty.

3. Think through every question you ask, first arguing against it as well as you can. For example, play devil's advocate about collecting telephone numbers. Why are you *requiring* your customers to reveal their phone numbers? Why, for that matter, require an email address? (There's probably a reason, but think it through. Think about the potential costs, not just the obvious potential marketing benefits.)

4. If you give people a persuasive *option* of providing private information, your best prospects will often be agreeable. After

that, the problem of sifting out bogus "required" data *(999-555-0505* and *lateralligator@getoutofmyface.com.usa.xxxy)* goes away.

5. Consider the supplemental use of live chat wherever possible and of prominently listed 800/888 numbers. This can keep people from being daunted by lengthy forms (and walking away) when they only wanted a bit of specific information. But don't let any of this stop you from providing a rapidly-answered email address as well. Note that some who approach your company online don't want to talk on the phone, no matter how friendly and well trained your "operators standing by" may be. Some are not even able to: The Internet has become an important tool for people with disabilities, including those with limited hearing, as well as for the inevitable stealthy at-work shoppers.

Fear Not: Don't Be Deterred from Collecting Information—Thoughtfully

Don't be deterred from collecting information—in a sensitive way, for respectful uses. There is little that's more important to your growth as a company. Indeed, effective tracking of what is important to customers—specific customers, not just customers in the aggregate—is a hallmark of all the excellent organizations we have worked with. It makes it possible for new staff to continue customer relationships built by departing or promoted colleagues as your company grows. It builds high, *sustainable* levels of customer loyalty.

It works for us.

We recommend it for you, too.

Building Anticipation *Into* Your Products and Services

Putting Processes to Work for You

Has Starbucks CEO Howard Schultz read *Catch-22*? Probably. What seems less likely is that Mr. Schultz has ever signed up for his own in-store Internet service.

Micah explains:

> I had some work to do while out of town, so I headed to Starbucks to try their new free WiFi.
>
> First step: I had to get a Starbucks card in order to sign up for free Internet. Okay, I guess. I purchased the card and filled in all of my personal information via my laptop. But then I got a message from AT&T/Starbucks Internet telling me to check my email account for an access verification code so I could complete the login process and begin using my new Internet account.
>
> Of course, I didn't *have* email access. *That's* why I bought the card and went through the sign-up process in the

first place. So in effect this message was telling me to drive home, check my email, click a link to get an access code, and then drive back to Starbucks.

We find a lot to admire in Howard Schultz. (One example: He's made it his personal mission to provide health-care benefits even to part-time workers.) But in this particular case, his company overlooked the following straightforward principle: *A business needs to think like a customer.* It needs to put in place processes that will mercilessly search and destroy anything that might inconvenience or disgruntle a customer. It must systematically incorporate procedures and build in product features that improve the customer's experience.

Let's look at how you go about this.

Get Your Company to Think Like a Customer

As a company, how do you learn what your customers are likely to appreciate—even before they arrive? You can start by making it clear throughout your company that it's your *goal* to learn. Then you can work with your employees to think systematically about particular groups of customers and what they are likely to want or need.

For example: Consider the plight of someone eating alone at a restaurant. Surrounded by chatty couples, groups, and families, the lone diner can feel socially awkward and a bit, well, lonely. Time passes more slowly. Food seems to take longer to arrive. What might make things less stressful for a guest in this situation?

Well, one thing you may notice is that those dining alone often bring, or hungrily grab, any available reading material. Bill Bryson recalls getting to the point of "reading restaurant placemats, then turning them over to see if there was anything on the back."[1]

Therefore, a thoughtful restaurant might establish as procedure to offer a choice of reading material, perhaps a newspaper or newsmagazine, to everyone who comes in to eat alone. That's a simple, considerate service rule that everybody on staff can implement.

Here are a few other examples of how you can anticipate customers' wishes with simple, thoughtful procedures:

➤ It's the middle of summer, and the customers who are entering your Atlanta boutique are escaping 95-degree heat. What would such customers likely want? Wouldn't they be pleased to find ice water with lemon slices on the counter when they walk in the door? You can easily establish this procedure as part of a daily weather-dependent setup.

➤ Do you know those signs that read, "If this restroom needs attention, please let us know" or, worse, the ones you see on airplanes that say, "It is not possible to clean up after every customer" and go on to suggest you sop up the basin with a hand towel as a courtesy to the next customer? The best procedural approach to restroom cleanliness probably isn't to install similar signs that put the onus on your customers for maintaining a clean facility. Here's a unique solution (in an admittedly rarefied setting): The staff at Charlie Trotter's famed restaurant in Chicago decided the only way to ensure its restrooms met the restaurant's standards, rather than leaving the next guest's experience at the whim of the last, was to *themselves* discreetly check the towels and soaps after every use.[2] (We don't necessarily recommend this extreme approach for you, except as a thought exercise; it's obviously a nonstarter if you run a crowded pub, for example. However, another proactive procedural approach—perhaps an attendant on busy nights—may be worth considering in such a situation.)

➤ What if you are on Taco Bell's executive team? Although your company's roots are So-Cal, if you're thinking like a customer, you'd fit watertight overhangs over your drive-through windows in most other locales. Customers in Sacramento might not care, but in Seattle don't you think they would prefer to skip the side order of soggy elbow and damp power window electronics?

It's important to build in mechanisms to ensure that company employees are frequenting your own physical and online facilities, because nothing is quite like the feedback you get this way. (By the way, if "company employees" currently means just yourself, still do your best to sample your own wares objectively, although achieving the anonymity we recommend below will be a stretch.)

We've all been to places where it seems no employee has ever eaten the food, attempted to reach the ill-placed toilet paper dispenser in the customer washroom, or noticed the way that items you're trying to purchase seem to vanish from the website's shopping cart. To avoid being one of these companies, *institutionalize* the internal, systematic use and testing of your own services or products. Offer deep discounts or comps for employee purchases, but with a string attached: If employees use your services, they must take detailed notes and—if this is realistic—remain anonymous, so they experience the same service other guests would.

Building procedural anticipation requires ongoing, daily effort. It requires managerial vision, judgment, and persistence. But it brings you closer to achieving customer loyalty.

Mr. BIV and the Art of Eliminating Defects

Sometimes problems *have* come up before and *have* been noticed by employees but are still hanging around. May we introduce you to Mr. BIV? When he's in charge, nothing ever changes.

Mr. BIV is a playful acronym coined by the group Leonardo worked with at The Ritz-Carlton. Addressing Mr. BIV helped them win two Malcolm Baldrige National Quality Awards. It remains one of the most useful—and easy to implement—quality improvement systems we've seen.

Mr. BIV is a streamlined, simplified, and easy-to-teach way to look for defects and defective situations; it can be adopted throughout an entire organization without requiring significant additional training. It stands for:

*M*istakes

*R*ework

*B*reakdowns

*I*nefficiencies

*V*ariation in work processes

Any employee, at any level of your organization, not only *may* but *must* alert the appropriate person to a Mr. BIV situation at once so it can be addressed right away. When Mr. BIV is encountered, it helps to ask "Why" as many as five times to reach the root cause rather than merely the symptom. For example:

Problem: Late room service

WHY? Waiters stuck waiting for elevator

WHY? Elevator monopolized by housemen

WHY? Housemen searching for/storing/hoarding linens

WHY? Shortage of linens

WHY? Inventory of linens only sufficient for 80 percent occupancy

You can deputize every employee as an "improvement manager" who is responsible for helping to implement the Mr. BIV system.

Mr. BIV represents a concise example of a *Continuous Improvement System*. The Continuous Improvement paradigm was developed in manufacturing industries, so, unfortunately, service, white collar, and "creative" professionals often make a knee-jerk assumption that it is not relevant to what they do. This is their great loss—and their customers', too. It doesn't really matter whether your product is electrical insulation, freelance editing, or wedding photography: You will only be able to *consistently* deliver a superb product when you have an effective system for monitoring and improving the product. That is why it would be hard to overstate the value of applying continuous improvement to the service aspects of your organization. It can close the competitiveness gap for a latecomer to a service industry or widen the distance between a standout service leader and the also-rans.

It's powerful stuff.

Don't Kill Mr. BIV's Messengers

Never attack employees for the problems that your Continuous Improvement System reveals. You need employees who are not scared or cynical: employees who are open about revealing defects. *A defect that happens twice should be assumed to be the fault of the process; the cure is in fixing the process.* If you attack your employees, they'll never help you find a recurring problem, and you won't have an early chance to fix the underlying defective process.

Eliminating Defects by Reducing Handoffs: Learning from Lexus

Leonardo recounts the story of how Toyota, with the assistance of Horst Schulze and other customer experience experts from varied disciplines, created the Lexus brand with the explicit goal of providing both an exceptional product and exceptional service interactions. Exceptional service was Lexus's best hope to build customer loyalty in an industry where loyalty traditionally comes only after multiple car purchases. (Only after you yourself had purchased a series of reasonably reliable Mercedes over more than a decade—typically three cars in a row—or, if it were a "family tradition" to own Mercedes—your grandfather drove a Mercedes, your father drove a Mercedes—could it be expected that your *future* purchases would be Mercedes. Toyota had no intention of waiting so long for its first crop of loyal Lexus customers.)

Lexus's final plan incorporated features we've addressed in earlier chapters, including greeting customers respectfully by name and unobtrusively logging and respecting individual customer preferences. But in addition, the company zeroed in on a strategy that we haven't discussed yet: reducing service defects through the minimization of "handoffs" between service providers.

In many contexts, lapses in service are most likely to occur when you are handing a customer over from one function, agent, or division to another. Have you ever had to re-explain yourself from the ground up when a phone service representative forwarded you to Technical Support? Whenever you transfer someone on the phone from one person to the next, there's a possibility of dropping the ball—of losing the phone connection or of failing to convey the information or the tenor of the situation along with the actual transfer. (Whenever an insurance salesperson hands the customer to the production department for service, that's where a problem is likely to happen. After a design client meets with the creative director, and the creative director then tries to convey the client information to the designer actually doing the job, that's where the ball is in danger of falling to the ground.)

This brings us to what a car customer typically experiences: You bring your car for service to a service department. There is a *person at the door* who greets you and takes you to the *service advisor*. The service advisor writes up what's wrong and calls the *mechanic*. The mechanic takes the car away. At the end, when it's time to pay the bill, the service advisor reappears, gives you the bill, and you have to go and deal with a disconnected, bored *cashier*, who is probably not focusing on you, not living up to service standards that match the car this same dealer sold you, and not capable of explaining what the strangely coded charges were for, because she wasn't even aware of your existence until this very moment.

Imagine instead that a single superbly trained service advisor, *Sharon*, takes care of you from the moment you enter the premises until the moment you leave the premises. *Sharon* greets you. *Sharon* writes up your service ticket. *Sharon* summarizes your complaint to the mechanic. *Sharon* alerts you when the car is ready. *Sharon* presents you with the bill, and *Sharon* accepts your payment. Lexus settled on this as their ideal approach, to be used to a greater or lesser extent depending on the size and other realities of a specific dealership.

Systematically Reducing Waste to Add Value—for You and Your Customers

Since we are fully committed *service* obsessives, you may be surprised at the extent to which we are fans of the best available *manufacturing*-based systems and controls. We've benchmarked and adopted approaches from companies as far-flung as Xerox, FedEx, and Milliken. And over and over, we've found insight in such manufacturing-centered systems as Lean Manufacturing and Total Quality Management.

For right-brain, high-touch service types, this probably sounds kind of like being forced to do homework. Yeah, it is kind of like that. And it's worth it.

These systems share the insight that *a company can increase its value by continually locating and trimming waste.* If applied appropriately, this emphasis can strengthen a service-centered company as much as it can a manufacturing concern. For example, we can speed up service response times by removing wasted time and motion; improve the variety of our offerings by having appropriately scaled processing equipment located throughout our facility; and enhance morale and profitability by reducing the time our staff spends waiting around. These examples, you may recognize, represent three of the seven classic "wastes" identified by Taiichi Ohno, father of the Toyota Production System, (the direct forerunner of today's Lean Manufacturing methodology):

➤ Unnecessary transport

➤ Excess inventory

➤ Excess and non-ergonomic motion

➤ Waiting

➤ Overproduction/ production ahead of demand

➤ Inappropriate processing

➤ Defects

Why Benchmark *Manufacturing* Companies?

To optimize efficiency, reliability, and delivery, we recommend you benchmark the wizards of manufacturing. Their successes come from the best kind of hard, scientific data, so learning from them can really tighten up your service ship. Concepts like *error-tolerant design* (for example, a door that won't let you lock yourself out accidentally), *behavior-shaping constraints* (e.g., a transmission that needs to be in "Park" before the key can be removed), and many other well-established concepts in manufacturing can bring advantages to your customers and your company, when applied appropriately in a service context.

To understand the value of applying manufacturing knowledge in a service context: Suppose you're planning a tapas bar in an exurb of Phoenix. You got the idea from your friend Joe, who developed the wildly successful *TapasTree* restaurant in Tucson. Joe got into the restaurant business to support his art collecting habits. Joe's been a kind of genius at creating an appealing, laid-back, artsy vibe in TapasTree's dining room. His approach is to think of dining out as an aesthetic experience, much like visiting an art museum or going to a gallery opening. Joe has taken that idea to its logical limits, by making his restaurant a "living gallery." Each seating enclave is in fact a unique sculptural ensemble, one that makes diners feel like they've been transported into a world where form and style transcend workaday concerns. And, wonderfully, the enclaves can be reconfigured in a matter of hours by a couple of waiters; the dining room's layout changes in marvelous ways from month to month.

This unique aesthetic really pulled people in. It gave Joe a huge head start in a low-margin business. Since his initial success, Joe has implemented a dozen other food-as-art insights in his restaurant, each of them capitalizing on his background as an art historian and connoisseur. After a year of rave reviews and paying off his initial debts, he's beginning to plan new locations.

In such a situation we'd certainly encourage you to explore whether aspects of Joe's success can be adapted if you're starting your own business—especially since Joe seems eager to be a model for you. But don't let him overreach his expertise. For example, we'd bet long odds that Joe hasn't mapped out an optimal kitchen workflow. And he has almost certainly missed some key inefficiencies that plague his supplier processes, among many others.

Of course, he doesn't realize he's wasteful in these areas; he figures his systems are optimized, battle-tested, the only way to go. (They are, after all, the only way he knows.) The bottom line? There's a lot to be learned studying the workflow ideas of the folks at Toyota, Cisco, or FedEx. Those are the go-to guys for streamlining and standardizing your behind-the-scenes operations—you might call them the professors of efficient and consistent outcomes. Joe's advice in these areas, on the other hand, may need to be taken with a big grain of *sal de mesa*.

Why Efficient Processes Can Transform Service

We understand why service-focused teams tend to be skeptical about the relevance of systems like Lean Manufacturing. After all, to stand out and inspire confidence, we strive to anticipate—to meet customers' needs *ahead* of time—because "just in time" can mean too darn late. We insist on keeping "excess" inventory, because it means we can maintain our high service standards (*"Absolutely, we've got that"*) even when unexpected demand occurs. We even encourage our employees to make "repetitive" motions on behalf of customers (*"Let me call the vendor again for you in an hour"*) precisely because willingness to be inefficient on their behalf is read by our customers as *caring*. More generally, we often need our employees to be "inefficient" in their caring for customers, because it enhances the customer's valuation of us.

Borrowing from Xerox

Years ago, we adopted a continuous improvement/problem-solving method that Xerox taught us when we were benchmarking them. The Xerox method is useful, especially in a team setting, when searching for solutions to wasteful situations and other business problems. It has just six parts. (Repeat if necessary until no longer needed.)

Step 1: Identify and select the problem to be worked on

Step 2: Analyze the problem

Step 3: Generate potential solutions

Step 4: Select and plan the best solution

Step 5: Implement the solution

Step 6: Evaluate the solution

For these reasons, our kind of enterprise seems more easily reconciled with a second principle of Lean Manufacturing: *Value is determined by your customers.* If it takes a thousand "inefficient" experiences to create loyal customers with confidence in us, so be it. Yes, it's slow, hard work to provide the kind of lavish, painstaking attention that produces unqualified positive reactions. But when our customers' satisfaction and loyalty are high, they value us highly. And when we're highly valued, we earn more. Hard measurements such as defect reduction metrics are important in service as well as in manufacturing, but there is something more here as well: In service-focused businesses, our customers don't tend to quantify the source of their happiness with precision. Instead, they come away from our efforts to serve them with a generalized glow, a vague feeling that they like us and want to return, and (we hope) a desire to tell their friends about us. That's the only sort of "value assessment" our loyal customers tend to assign to our superb service.

So can the "efficiency increases value" concept really help us serve our customers better? It can, we believe—so long as you restrict its territory a bit. We *do* want to be highly efficient—especially *behind the scenes*. For example, to return to our hypothetical friend TapasTree Joe, the continuous motion of the Lean Manufacturing approach could well bring him dramatic improvement over traditional batch-and-queue prep, with its wasteful down times interspersed with chaotic scenes of yelling chefs and frantic "expediting." Improving behind-the-scenes efficiency also serves our customers well by reducing errors, improving delivery time, and keeping staff fresh and alert.[3]

Similarly, in online commerce, behind-the-scenes streamlining of customer choices through analysis of customer patterns increases value for company and customer alike, as long as it is not intrusive. And if online customers want to proverbially "help out in the back" by doing their own account management, this can increase your efficiency and help you provide faster service at a lower price. We recommend such self-service be voluntary in most business contexts, or that you at least include systems that monitor customer frustration levels and provide them with many escape hatches—like effective, well-staffed online support chat and a toll-free hotline, just in case they get stuck.

Stamping Out Waste? Don't Crush Value by Accident

We wish all of our clients had a giant red "pause" button they could push whenever they get the urge to purge customer service processes, procedures, and traditions accumulated over years of service. Our concern is born of experience: Service-focused companies tend to delete crucial value from their service offerings, all in the name of efficiency. When they realize what they've lost, it's too late. Starting to think that your follow-up thank-you cards aren't valuable to customers? Or that your original ink signature on letters to incoming customers is a waste of your time? Or that your customers won't notice if you drop a website feature they rarely use? You may be right. But don't do anything yet. Because the odds are pretty good that you're underestimating the value of the old approach to your customers. Here's why.

First, people form *emotional attachments* to many aspects of their lives—including attachments to your employees, your procedures, and your service features. Emotional attachments are by their nature not rational. If you repeatedly experience delight in a particular context (at work, in a relationship, in your summers on the Cape), you'll tend to form an emotional attachment to many aspects of that context. A child happily raised in and accustomed to a room with yellowing walls—surfaces which were originally white—may not react to a gleaming white repainting of it with the gratitude her parents expected.

In the same way, aspects of your service that seem expendable to you, and thus "wasteful" to retain, may have come to have emotional value for some of your customers. To make matters worse, even interviews with your most articulate customers may fail to register accurately the depth of their attachment to, say, being greeted by the smell of fresh coffee in your reception area in the mornings—because the strength of long-term emotional attachments tends to be underestimated, until it's too late. Ever been surprised how much you missed a sweetheart after being sure it was time to break up? Then you know what we're talking about.

A more general problem is that people usually aren't paying close attention to their positive experiences, and therefore don't know what *specific* aspects of their experience felt especially good to them. When you ask people to think back on an experience, they try to come up with "a theory of why I liked/disliked it"—which is what you asked them to do, after all. But one of the best-tested findings in social psychology is that *while people do have accurate access to their feelings, their theories about why they feel the way they do can be wildly inaccurate.* People are especially poor at detecting the origins of their *positive* feelings. The bottom line? Even very intelligent and well-intentioned customers can lead you astray if asked to, say, "List the five things that make you feel the best during your encounters with us." So don't be too quick to delete things that didn't make their top lists.

Try this exercise sometime: Ask a friend to think back on a great dining experience she had, even as recently as a couple months ago. Then cross-examine her:

Do you remember the décor of the place?
Not precisely.
Do you remember the face of the waiter?
No, I can't.
Do you remember the face of the maitre d'?
Nope.
What did you have for an appetizer?
I can't quite remember.
What did you have for an entrée?
I can't quite remember.
What did you have to drink?
I can't quite remember.
Was there anything special about the valet parking?
I can't remember.
Then what was so great about it?
I don't know exactly, but it was a great experience.

Using Lean Manufacturing's methodology (that only what is valued by the customer has value), everything above, taken *individually*, could easily be thrown into the classification of *muda* (waste): the excellence of the valet parker (for all the description you got, your friend might have taken the bus), the faceless maitre d' (she could have seated herself); the faceless server (a buffet would have been very practical); even the excellent quality of the food, wine, and décor, none of which she remembered in much detail. Yet all of these touch points, and so many more, ultimately built an experience that was more than the sum of its parts: The *collective* is what does it. That's why the attention to details is so important in the service business: making sure that each one of those touch points is well executed.

By the way, we could make an educated guess as to the details that added up, bit by bit, to your friend's appraisal of having had a "fabulous" night out. Let's analyze just the last touch point in question (which, as a hello/good-bye [see Chapter 11] is one of the most likely to have left an impression): We like to think the valet parker greeted her, smiled at her, and was prompt. He didn't walk to retrieve her car, he ran. This action signaled subliminally that he cared—that he was committed to giving her prompt service. He took time to wipe her windshield. He did not change her radio station. He did not move her seat in a way that required her to readjust it, or if he did need to adjust her seat, he at least showed concern about the inconvenience: *"Ma'am, I had to move your seat."*

Service Alfresco

To create a fresco requires a palette of colors, skill, time, and attention—and the judgment and foresight to envision a painting that will fit just right on a particular wall. To create exceptional service, treat every single time you come in contact with your customers as an opportunity to add another brush stroke to their service fresco.

A great service provider is always looking for an opportunity to pull out the palette and add a few more touches that will make a more vivid, inspiring impression. In the face of the struggle to reduce waste, a great service provider knows these extra touches, as long as they actually reach the customer, are never wasted. They're what keep a business the picture of good health.

Process-Based Anticipation on the Internet

When you interact with customers via the Internet, you have an opportunity to provide anticipatory service created or enhanced by software algorithms—algorithms that offer individualized guidance and assistance to your customers. The best of these anticipatory algorithms can help a

customer make sophisticated service or purchasing decisions by analyz-
ing the preferences of past customers who have behaved in the same
ways as the current one, as well as taking into account how the customer himself has behaved in earlier interactions on the site.

The Netflix online video rental site is an example of an unusually
sophisticated, algorithm-based procedure. Netflix's algorithms are based
on millions of previous customer actions. The algorithms allow Netflix
to accurately predict which movies will appeal to a particular customer
as soon as that user begins selecting and rating movies. The software can
even make rather impressive educated guesses *before* a customer makes a
first selection by weighing such variables as the customer's gender, zip
code, and initial "search style" on the website.

Humans appear to be wired to respond appreciatively to anticipatory service. That's why Netflix's ability to figure out a customer's preferences feels so impressive. Indeed, regular customers describe a sense
of having a "relationship" with the Netflix website; it feels to them as
though the site "knows" them personally. That's how Netflix creates
intense customer loyalty—it's one of the best-loved customer service
sites on the Internet—despite providing customers with not even a single moment of direct human interaction in the course of a typical encounter.

But before you rush to become the Netflix of your industry, remember our discussion in Chapter Five of how easy it is to cross a line
from "ultra-functionality" to "creepiness" online. Given the creepiness
factor, should online retailers make personalized purchase suggestions
based on the behaviors already traced to a customer's IP address, or
should they wait until the customer has voluntarily logged in? It's
tempting to push the envelope, isn't it? After all, if you logged and
analyzed *all* of a customer's behaviors on your website, you could probably make your website more relevant for them.

But consider the downside: Do your customers *want* to have their
behavior tracked even before they log into your site? And do you want
to risk potential side effects, such as inadvertently offering children sug-

gestions for lacy, barely-there things based on some browsing their parents did in anticipation of Valentine's Day?

Our opinion is that a committed service provider needs to make the decision to actually serve its customers' interests—not just *seem* to serve them. So modulate your use of online anticipatory technology. Steer your company practices away from that creepiness line.

Using Tools to Gather Information About Your Customers' Experience

There are many tools available to help you build the viewpoint of your customers into each of your products and services. Consider making use of one or more of the following: mini-customer surveys ("quizzes"), in-depth surveys, and possibly secret shopper services to gather information about the typical customer experience.

In-House "Quizzes." An on-site, three-to-seven-question mini-survey, or "quiz," tends to yield a very high participation rate. This rate is typically much higher than for a survey sent after customers have returned home and much higher than a full-length survey, whether offered onsite or later.

In-Depth Surveys. In-depth surveys can be useful to any company, no matter how small. If your company is large enough to generate survey data of some magnitude, these surveys should be administered and analyzed scientifically. This may be best done in collaboration with a specialized outside service. However you decide to handle them, be sure to remain involved in their design and administration, because there's no point in a survey that gives you plenty of answers—but to the wrong questions! Consider the following points:

➤ A survey should reflect your most important questions about customer likes, dislikes, and needs. A good survey question is clearly worded and directly explains what you are trying to find out.

➤ A survey should include free-form text fields to identify novel responses that you may not have even considered and to offer your customers an opportunity to express themselves.

➤ Questions and introductory material on a survey should be designed to give you meaningful responses. Asking a customer to be a mathematician ("Estimate your chances of returning to our store this month in terms of percentage of 100 . . .") will create confusion and frustration. Asking your customer several individual questions and only *then* getting around to asking for an overall rating is the exact wrong order, and invalidates the overall rating. Ask for the overall rating *first*, since it's the single most important rating, reflecting a gut reaction. Concluding your survey with language such as "Thank you so much for entrusting us with your business!" helps you to end up with customers who are on your side, but don't use this flowery language as an intro—it'll skew your rating. Don't use rating categories like "excellent"; "excellence" is essentially undefinable, so look for something that is based on your customer's own experience. "Exceeded expectations" is okay as the wording for your top rating category, or consider calling your top rating something emotive like "Loved it!"

➤ Two questions that are especially useful proxies for loyalty are "intent to return" and "willingness to recommend" your business. Top scores in these two areas are strong indicators of a loyal customer.

➤ As you might suspect from where you've been with us so far, in our experience the number of so-called "top box" scores (the highest raters, especially highest raters on the key "intent to return" and "willingness to recommend" questions) you receive on your surveys is more important to your brand than the average or overall satisfaction score you get by tabulating all your surveys. In other words, customers who rate you in the absolute top category are the ones who are adding the strategic value to your business. *These* are your loyalists. Put another way, with a properly designed survey, you should be happier to receive a sizeable chunk of tens (if that's your top score) with a smattering of fours than to receive solid sevens across the board. The sevens are not loyalists and are not going to sing the praises of your brand from the rooftops. Furthermore, with the mad skills you're learning from this book, you're not going to let that smattering of fours scare you: you're going to reach out to them pronto and work on winning them over and getting them up to a ten before they fill out another survey.

Six Survey Blunders: How to Alienate Customers Fast

1. Neglecting to respond *personally* and *promptly* after receiving negative feedback. When you receive negative survey comments, respond quickly by telephone (this is best in most cases) or email; this is a situation where a handwritten note takes too long to arrive and can leave a customer stewing in the interim. Don't set a batch of surveys aside for later en masse response without scanning them first for negative responses that require immediate replies.

2. Failing to thank—again, *personally*—anyone who offers you personal praise on a survey. A handwritten note is wonderful in this case.

3. Providing a reward for a completed survey that doesn't fit with your company's image or a sweepstakes chance so unrealistically small as to be meaningless. (Rather than offering either of these, it would be better to simply say, "We really want to improve—please take this survey to help us out if you'd be so kind.")

4. Asking customers to be on an "advisory council" or hold a similar honorary position . . . and then only contacting them with obvious come-ons.

5. Creating a survey that is too much work to fill out, with no opportunity to answer a short form or skip any portions of the long survey. (Do you really only want to know the preferences of customers who took the time to answer a thirty-question survey without leaving a single answer blank?)

6. Asking intrusive demographic questions (such as income or gender) and not making the questions optional. Do not assume that respondents will trust your privacy practices.

Secret Shoppers. Professional "secret shoppers" will anonymously patronize your business and describe the experience to you in detail. For some businesses, this can be invaluable. The fact that a critical review comes from a complete outsider is very helpful to some organizations. Members of an organization respond differently to criticism from somebody outside of their social and power hierarchies—someone who presumably has no dog in the fight. Some employees find it easier to accept truths about their service shortcomings, and to get right to work making important changes, when the news comes from a secret shopper service.

On the other hand, as with outside survey services, a secret shopping firm needs to know what you want it to test for. What's important to your business may be very specific and contextually subtle. So the generic checklist used as a default by an outside service is unlikely to be useful. Instead, you will need to work with them to ensure that they are after what *you* are after.

Steering a Company Is Easier with a (3-D) Dashboard

You could, in theory, drive a car without a dashboard. But sooner or later you'd be caught speeding, or run out of gas, or burn up the engine—all hazards that indicators on a dashboard would have signaled far in advance. A company also needs a dashboard: a complement of highly visible meters and early warning signs that protect against foreseeable problems.

The kind of dashboard we recommend includes more than traditional "hard" measurements. Steering your company while only looking at such measurements is kind of like running a business by only looking at your checkbook (*"Hey, I'm not over-*

drawn right now, so everything must be fine."); it's a unidimensional way to manage a business. The simplicity of the dashboard concept can be used instead to bring the richness of what's important to the forefront. So, while your dashboard will include the so-called "hard" indicators of corporate health like throughput, revenue, and expenditures, at least as important will be indicators such as employee engagement, problem resolution success, and customer loyalty. (Are you losing or gaining in the number of customers willing to refer your business and who are planning to use your business again? Your dashboard should provide these answers at a glance.) These "softer" indicators can be derived from your preferred tracking tools—your customer "quizzes," surveys, secret shopper reports, and employee-filed reports, as well as data gathered on employee engagement by your managers and HR leaders.

Process-Based Solutions Become People Solutions

When you are able to anticipate a customer's wishes, it implies that you are paying close, caring attention, the kind of attention that is a universal, if often unexpressed, desire. In many industries, what you're primarily selling is this pleasure of attention: rich, personal attention. Ironically, the thing that's most expensive to provide customers—a defect-free product—just gets you in the door. Only human attention is going to differentiate you and win your customer's loyalty.

You don't need to have a luxury brand or serve a specialized clientele to build loyalty through anticipatory service—although the details of how you should attend to the wishes of customers will vary with the expectations and cultural norms of your customers themselves. For example, it is expected and necessary for staff at a Disney park to provide *briskly paced* attentiveness. Contrast that with the slow, luxurious attentiveness of a high-end spa. In our experience, all businesses can benefit from building an anticipatory service culture—from golf courses to Google—and even to a gas station.

Think of a fellow who buys his gas at the local service station—let's call it DinoFuels—many mornings. He's a *habitual* customer: It's convenient for him to stop there on the way to work. But if he's coming *from* the office, he's not going to go to all of the trouble of making a half-mile U-turn in order to patronize that particular service station. If it's not perfectly convenient, he'll fill up somewhere else.

Is there anything that DinoFuel's friendly, personable attendant could do to turn this habitual customer into a loyal one? Put differently: What costs almost nothing, yet would make this hurried gentleman go half a mile out of his way in order to shop there in the future for gas, and for higher-margin items like milk, eggs, snacks—even a tune-up?

We encourage our clients to role-play this scenario, to figure out what procedures DinoFuels could institute to turn *them* into loyal customers. Let's let Leonardo lead by example here by playing the role of the customer:

> The attendant should be keeping an eye out for customers who are becoming habitual customers: customers who are frequent, but not quite loyal. If he's doing that, he'll be aware of my repeat business. Then he could note the name on those customers' credit cards—since nearly everyone pays for gas with credit cards these days—and at the very least use my name when thanking me. If he's up to the task, he might take it much further. Something like:

> *"Oh, that's an interesting name. How do you pronounce it?"*
> "Ing-hill-AIR-ee," I would say.
> *"That's a nice name. Where are you from?"*
> "I was born in Italy."
> *"Italy, wow! Italy looks so lovely in the pictures I've seen. Where in Italy were you born?"*
> "I was born in Rome. And where are you from?"

"I was born in Jamaica."

"Jamaica's such a great island. I've been on a vacation there,
   Montego Bay area. Is that near where you come from?"

"I was born closer to Kingston."

And yappedy, yappedy, yappedy, yap.

If all goes well, the attendant will have established an emotional
connection in this conversation. So the next time Leonardo pulls in to
the station, what might the attendant do? He might say something like:

"Leonardo, welcome back! I haven't seen you for a while.
Have you been in Europe?"

"No, I was just in New York for a few days visiting
friends."

"And these friends you were visiting: Are they Italian,
too?"

"Oh no, no, they come from Philadelphia."

"Oh, then I'm sorry for them," he could reply, smiling.

A service station seems like a mundane setting, yet this attendant
has just provided anticipatory service. He has gone to the trouble to
remember the customer's name, preferences, and life history. Because
being attended to is a nearly universal human desire, the attendant's
behavior likely constitutes the anticipation of Leonardo's unexpressed
wishes. In consequence, the customer is likely to begin to have loyal
feelings toward this attendant and, more generally, toward the attendant's employer, DinoFuels. Keep this relationship going, and soon
Leonardo *will* bother to make a half-mile U-turn in rush hour traffic in
order to shop there.

Once he's loyal, the customer will also become more forgiving of
occasional lapses in service at Dino. This is an important advantage of
cultivating loyal customers. When a merely satisfied customer encounters one of your mistakes, positive feelings you've built up in that cus-

tomer reset to zero—at best. In contrast, now that this particular customer feels emotionally attached to DinoFuels, the station's staff can make some flubs without erasing his built-up feelings of goodwill toward them.

Volume Is No Excuse: Let's Get the Process Started

The typical excuse for not trying to recall individuals and their preferences or idiosyncrasies is "volume": "We serve too many customers to set up a process that requires us to remember them individually." This is a questionable excuse, but we hear it regularly even from businesses with a more limited customer base (and far greater upside per customer) than a gas station, such as law firms. It's true that the on-the-fly remembering and acknowledgement of minor customer details in a situation like this is dependent on individual employees. So a reasonable question is: How many individual customers, for example, can *you* "remember"? We're confident that the answer is in the hundreds. It's not that you have to remember every single detail of their lives—just a few minor points. (Of course, for more complex use of customer details and preferences, we advocate computer-aided memory systems, as discussed in Chapter 5.)

Let's assume you are indeed hard at work in a gas station, with twelve busy pumps. You have about ten customers per pump per hour. That is 120 brief transactions an hour, about 960 customers per eight-hour shift. Many customers pay at the pump, which leaves you probably interacting with a few hundred people a day. Perhaps 25 percent of these are the habitual customers our proposed process suggests you interact with: probably fifty people a day, in this very busy business. And, of course in almost any business, the demand will be even less than this.

But you need to get the process started.

The balance of the transition from habitual to loyal depends on people skills: on employees who are hired, trained, and inspired to excel at anticipatory service. (To give just one example, the attendant would need the finesse to know not to engage Leonardo this actively if Leonardo had shown signs of restlessness or wanting to be left alone.) Finding, training, and inspiring such people is a central issue, with rewarding solutions, and we're about to get into it elbow-deep.

Take a breath. We're ready when you are.

CHAPTER SEVEN

Your People

Selection, Orientation, Training, and Reinforcement

The art of anticipation requires, at its core, the right people. People who have been chosen correctly for their positions, who understand their purpose in your organization, who are inspired by leadership, trained in the necessary technical skills, and given reinforcement daily.

Let's take a closer look.

We Are Already Our True Selves: Select for Traits

How can you fill the ranks of your company with people who will be superb at anticipating the needs of your customers? To begin with, you need to move away from hiring in most positions for specific *skills* and toward selecting for *talent*. Give that friendly, insightful, responsible applicant who has a knack for making people feel comfortable a shot—even if it means passing over an applicant with a résumé that more closely matches the job's day-to-day functions.

Why? Although we all want to believe that our personality traits and aptitudes can shift at any time throughout our lives, such change rarely happens in adulthood. Decades of research have consistently shown that most of us persist throughout adult life with more or less the same personalities and aptitudes with which we began it. So if Jane has always tended to become quarrelsome under stress, she'll probably have that tendency throughout the decades ahead of her. If Jack is now a superbly patient and supportive listener, he's very likely going to stay that way until his dotage.

Can we be certain that any particular employee will conform to this rule? Absolutely not. But successful businesses are built on a series of well-calculated bets, not guarantees. And your likeliest bet is that your employees have already settled into the personalities and aptitudes that they'll have in the future. Remember this whenever you are selecting representatives of your brand, and you'll come out ahead. Recognize this, and you'll understand why we recommend using the best personality and aptitude assessment tools available to you—appropriate testing, appropriate evaluation—to find people with the talents you're looking for.

Isn't it important to hire the applicant with the best job-specific experience? Quite often, the answer is no. Job functions can be taught, but it's nearly impossible to teach empathy, energy, or cognitive flexibility. So go ahead and set up your hiring process around lifelong traits such as a sincere and pleasant way of interacting with other people, a good command of language, a sense of responsibility and commitment, and so forth. Generate your own list of the traits that are crucial to your business.

Here are the top five traits we have found to be the most important for the people we select to join us in our enterprises. We find these five traits useful in selecting candidates for a service position from a hospital to a bank, from a tech support counter to a call center that serves an online florist.

1. *Genuine personal warmth.* Ask men and women what they want in a spouse, and they'll tell you slightly different things. But interestingly, in survey after survey, men and women from various cultures agree on the single most important characteristic: *warmth*. Genuine warmth (or, as it is sometimes called, *kindness*) in a mate is valued more than any-

thing else. It even trumps physical attractiveness, compatibility of interests, or success. From infancy onward, warmth serves to reassure us that somebody won't double-deal us, turn on us, or abandon us in our moment of need.

People are hard-wired to pick up on warmth, or its absence, very quickly. They're also excellent at detecting phony warmth *simulations*. That's one reason why it's foolish to hire cold or stand-offish representatives in the hope of training them to *act* warmly with customers. Customers, like people everywhere, are superb at detecting counterfeit warmth.

2. Empathic skill. Warmth and empathic skill are interrelated, but it's helpful to know the difference between them and to make sure that both are represented in your employees. One way to think about the difference: Warmth involves a tendency to express sincerely positive feelings toward people. Empathic skill is the ability to understand what another human being is going through and how to interact helpfully in that situation.

An example: Joan is a company employee with abundant warmth but low empathic skill. Because of her warmth, we know she will *want* to say exactly the right thing when a long-term client blurts out that he just lost his job. But without strong empathic skill, she won't know which kinds of reactions are likely to be helpful, which are likely just to be awkward, and which are likely to actually cause the poor fellow more pain.

Now Kevin, who works in the same company as Joan, has high warmth *and* high empathic skill. He cares about his clients, but he also knows when to avoid a personal topic, when to offer an opinion, and when to just ask gentle questions. Kevin almost certainly would have been able to help the same client feel understood, supported, and gently encouraged.

3. An optimistic, upbeat attitude. Service can be draining. This is true when you're learning the ropes, and it's still true when you've been in the business a long time. Setbacks are common, reversals of fortune occur—and if you are inclined to a pessimistic view of things, you won't be able to snatch victory from the jaws of defeat. Psychologist Martin E. P. Seligman has studied the importance of positive attitude in business. Seligman's research shows that in many positions, including those he calls "high burnout jobs," the single most important difference between success and failure is not intelligence, luck, or experience. It is whether employees have an "optimistic explanatory style"[1] or a pessimistic one. That's because a pessimistic attitude *("That customer doesn't really want to hear from me")* tends to become a self-fulfilling prophecy *("I can't call on that customer out of the blue now—we haven't spoken in months, and she's probably taken her business to another company.")*

How employees understand causation helps determine performance in service positions. Consider Kevin, the employee with considerable warmth and empathetic skill. If Kevin is also an optimist, he will avoid feeling demoralized by a customer who takes out frustrations on him— and therefore he'll find it easier to snap back and regroup later in the workday. When an order goes awry for a customer, a more pessimistic service professional may become paralyzed by fear—not only for his client's well-being, but for his own.

(However, it is important to have some of the potentially adaptive aspects of pessimism represented within your company ranks as well. Pessimism can positively lead to: thinking things through to avoid errors, inhibiting impulsive or brash actions, and not being easily satisfied that "everything is great now." Excessive optimism can be downright dangerous in certain positions in any organization: from financial forecaster to safety officer to professional driver. There is no one profile that is going to fit every position within an organization.)

4. A team orientation. It's easy now to imagine our Kevin interacting warmly, insightfully, and optimistically with a discouraged client. But suppose that Kevin is poor at keeping others on his team informed about how the client is doing, rejecting any offers of support in meeting her service needs *("You know I can handle it all myself").* Kevin's work style is likely to cause trouble on any tightly interrelated team. If Kevin lacks the teamwork trait, he will wreak havoc on his teammates.

5. *Conscientiousness.* Conscientiousness is a broad trait that subsumes concepts like responsibility, work ethic, diligence, and attention to getting the details right. The conscientious employee takes pride in doing things well, pays close attention to his work, stays organized, and follows through. All the warmth, empathy, optimism, and team spirit in the world won't suffice if you lack conscientiousness. A client of a representative like that will say things like this: *"Yes, Kevin has been wonderfully encouraging. He really seems to understand my priorities, and he has helped me connect with some terrific resources. But I've had a lot of trouble reaching him, he tends not to reply to my emails for days, he forgets to do even the most basic things, and, to cap it all off, he called today to say he's lost my file! I'm sorry, I've had it."*

Whatever combination of trait criteria you settle on, you'll need to vigorously defend and promote its use, especially when your company is growing quickly. Others will pressure you at such times to fill positions regardless, without slowing down. Resist.

Keep the Hiring Bar High

Resist the temptation to fill a vacant position with an inferior employee. In the strange-but-true department, in most cases it is better to have a team of superb employees suffer temporary overload than to insert ill-suited employees into the team. This is a very hard principle for service-oriented people to accept, since we want, for example, the phones answered quickly. Yes, that *is* important! But a single bad recruit can poison the mood of an otherwise effective team. The more significant the position, the greater the dose of poison you administer.

Over and over, we've watched an entire team's performance sink when a single wrong employee is hired. To understand why, imagine a group of runners that gets together every Sunday evening. The members of our group have varied paces. Marty is fast, with a six-minute, thirty-second pace. Wanda runs a seven-minute, thirty-second pace—very quick. Leonardo runs at eight minutes, thirty seconds, and Ezra runs a nine-minute pace. What is the speed of our group? It's the speed of the slowest runner in our group: Ezra's nine-minute pace. Sooner or later, Marty's going to say, *"Hey, nine minutes is too slow. I'm out of here."* He'll go somewhere else and find a new group of runners that runs a pace closer to his. It's similar in business: When you hire an ill-suited employee, you don't just slow down your business. You drive away your best-performing employees as well.

You may also drive away your best customers. Whenever you put together a mostly, but not consistently, excellent team, customers will usually interact with at least one sub-par employee. And we know that customers tend to judge firms by the *weakest* links they encounter in the customer service chain. That's why even a few poor brand representatives can jeopardize your hard-earned customer loyalty.

Develop Selection Discipline

Developing an effective interview and selection process takes discipline. Many businesses make use of science-based employee selection services. Leonardo often makes use of the interview design resources from a company called Talent Plus, and Micah's has seen good results with the Caliper system. As with outside survey resources, the best results are obtained when the outside organization or system accommodates your company's own hiring criteria.

Whichever selection approach you decide is right for you, consider incorporating internal *personnel benchmarking*. This means that you systematically compare each new applicant's profile to those of your own best performers and those of your standard performers, to see how they match up. (You won't have this detailed personnel benchmarking data initially. You can build it up over time and incorporate it into your selection processes as it grows.)

Once you settle on a scientific approach to employment screening, don't just use it as "seasoning"—sprinkling a bit here or there as the mood strikes you, and skipping it when it doesn't suit you. Whatever selection process you set up must be used with *every* recruit; otherwise you will never know how effective your tool is and what work may be needed to hone it.

Create a Powerful Orientation Process

Do you know—for certain—what the first day of work is like for your employees? Is there a chance it runs something like this?

> The chief technician at the body shop looks at his new employee and says, "Welcome to our shop. What's your name again? Jim? Oh, okay. Yes, welcome to our shop, Jim. Let me see your uniform, yeah; your shoes, okay. Do you have a pen, pencil, pad? Yep, you have everything. Okay, follow Bill. He'll show you everything that goes on in this shop."
>
> So, the new employee follows Bill, who has been disgruntled ever since he was demoted in '02 because of his poor work ethic. Since then, Bill's favorite job duty has been orienting new recruits. Out of earshot of the boss, he smiles wanly at Jim. "Let me tell you how it *really* works around here . . ."

Around the world each day, careless orientations like this one are creating lasting negative expectations among employees. And executives and managers typically have no idea it's happening. Be sure your precious first moments with an employee aren't squandered (or worse). Institute a careful, effective orientation process.

Use Orientation to Instill New Values, Attitudes, and Beliefs

Employees are especially impressionable during their first days—and especially their *very first day*—on the job. This is because beginning any new job is disorienting, and psychologists have shown that during periods of disorientation, people are particularly susceptible to adopting new roles, goals, and values. Those new values and beliefs might turn out to be subversive ones like Bill was trying to plant, or constructive ones like you want to seed. It depends largely on your orientation program.

With this in mind, we recommend that you focus your orientation process not on instilling practical know-how, but rather on instilling the most useful possible attitudes, beliefs, and goals. Keep the focus on what is most crucial for your business: core customer service principles, your company values, and why and how your employee is an essential part of the company's overall mission. Don't fritter away orientation on in-consequential details. *("This is the break room. We clean the employee fridge out each Friday.")*

Involve the highest leadership level possible, ideally the CEO, to personally provide the orientation on values, beliefs, and purpose. Sound impractical, even impossible? Consider this: Horst Schulze personally conducted every Day One orientation at every new Ritz-Carlton hotel and resort that opened worldwide, throughout his tenure. He now continues this tradition at the Capella and Solis hotels and resorts.

So, figure out a way. You only get one Day One.

Defining an Employee's Underlying Purpose

A particularly crucial aspect of orientation is ensuring that a new employee understands her particular *underlying purpose* in your organization and appreciates its importance. An object can only have a function. A human being has both a function—his day-to-day job responsibilities—and a purpose—the reason why the job exists. (For example, "To create a memorable experience for our guests" is the purpose we hope will move our engineer off the ladder at the beginning of this book.)

If an employee understands that she has an underlying essential purpose in your company, she'll tend to respond to customers differently. Among other things, she'll try harder to comprehend what they need and to come up with creative ways to meet their needs. This can be a huge asset when confusing or stressful service situations arise, including situations that have never been planned for.

Even in a mundane situation, this simple understanding, starting from day one, can make all the difference. Have you ever been to a shopping mall and stared, obviously bewildered, at the map—while a security guard idly stands there "protecting" you, all of two feet away? Did the security guard proactively help you out with an *"Anything I can help you find?"* If he worked for us, he would have. At orientation, we would have started him off understanding his higher purpose: *to create a great shopping experience for guests.* Sure, that could include deterring and apprehending bad guys, but it also includes attending to shoppers who have that unmistakable lost look on their faces.

The Orientation Process Begins Sooner Than You Think

The orientation process begins the moment an employee is told she's been hired. From that point onward, every interaction with this incoming staffer will influence her beliefs about your company. So think carefully about all contact with the new recruit, including form letters your company sends her, how she is treated when she calls with a question about benefits, and so forth.

Orientation should then move into the emotionally compelling Day One component, a separate event that marks a dividing line between the past and the future. This conveys an important message: Your work life, your assumptions, even your values at work, are going to be different from this point forward.

On Day One, Nothing Is Tangential

Even seemingly peripheral aspects of your orientation program can influence a new employee's relationship with your company. To get a first-hand appreciation for how important these aspects of orientation can be, suppose for a moment that you're on the receiving end of orientation. You're excited to be newly hired as a junior vice president. That is, until the day you report to work and find you don't have an active company phone line, a computer login, business cards, or most of the other tools you need. Yet they've known you were coming for three months: plenty of time to get your business cards, your company ID, your company credit card, your parking spot: all the helpful, practical items to get you up and running. You can already tell that the first week is going to be a week in limbo, and it's raising questions in your mind about the company you've signed on with. *Your orientation is already going badly before the scheduled sessions have even begun.*

Now suppose that on Day One, the most influential day of your new job, you are wedged into a messy meeting room and given cock-eyed photocopies-of-photocopied handouts, asked to read them under buzzing fluorescent bulbs, and surrounded by strewn-about computer equipment. You're now subliminally absorbing the kind of messages that lead to customers getting substandard, out of date, poorly aligned, messy service. Some orientation! It's hard under such circumstances not to feel cynical about the speech from the senior vice president about the company's "paramount value of excellence."

So when it's *your* turn to be in charge, avoid conditioning employees negatively. Practice your Day One comments in front of a critical colleague until you can consistently deliver them superbly. Prepare the orientation rooms perfectly, with all the chairs tucked in straight, perfectly aligned, everything clean, and all the visuals effectively prepared. Offer simple refreshments—piping hot coffee, fresh cookies—perfectly arranged. Use only good-quality, closely edited, and up-to-date handouts. (Go ahead and splurge: Print out fresh copies.)

Build a Brand Ambassador

After the emotion and drama of Day One, you settle into the long process of building the necessary skills for the new employee to perform the job. Most importantly, you initiate the "brand ambassador" process: the process that transforms a new recruit into an effective representative for your company. How long that takes depends on the nature of the brand, the particular employee, and the employee's position. Building a brand ambassador can take two months, three months, six months, or a year. But it's certainly not a one-week, two-week, or zero-week process.

Never permit a new employee to represent you in interactions with customers before he has completed your orientation process. Customers never deserve to be practiced on. The only exception to this is the "following" of another employee by a trainee, clearly represented as such, while the veteran being followed protects the customer from any negative impact.

Everyone's an Expert

We recommend that current non-managerial employees (not just HR employees, but operational employees) participate in departmental recruiting, selection, hiring interviews, and orientation. (Note that your relationship with an applicant is legally sensitive, so you need to do this with some care, and your employees will need training and supervision as they assume such responsibilities.) For any service-minded employee on your team, the chance to be involved in hiring instills a sense of pride in, engagement with, and commitment to the organization. By promoting a positive vision of the company to new recruits, and by working on selecting those recruits, your staff will naturally invest themselves more in the company's mission. So it's a terrific investment of your supervisory time and energy.

Training Employees to Anticipate . . . *Carefully*

A key component of building a superb service team is *teaching*. You need to make a significant, ongoing investment in teaching your employees the skills they need to do their jobs properly. Business types usually call the teaching they do *training*. But training is just a variant of teaching.

If you've observed any teachers closely, you know that theirs is a much tougher job than it seems from afar. Their students only turn into knowledgeable, versatile experts after weeks of intensive, guided learning. The work of a business trainer is tough, too. Effective, consistent service professionalism only emerges after hours of expert instruction, coaching, and guided practice.

There's no way around the difficulties and hassles that excellent training involves, but it is truly worth all the time and trouble. A commitment to and understanding of proper training is a golden ticket in an increasingly competitive marketplace. Few businesses and business leaders show the doggedness needed to commit to, structure, and maintain the training needed to create and sustain a superb service staff. If you have that tenacity and vision, it will help your company lead its field.

The Passion for Training

Starting in the Middle Ages, master craftsmen would bring in young apprentices and teach them a craft—a process that took the better part of a decade. Nowadays it may seem anachronistic to emphasize lengthy, intensive training amid so much preoccupation with efficiency and speed. But it's an important leadership responsibility to ensure proficiency, and the patient, deliberate skill transfer from master to apprentice has huge value. Great organizations understand that they must be "learning organizations": they learn from their customers, from their employees, and from their competitors. Great organizations are also "training organizations." Otherwise, what will happen to all that organizational learning?

We recommend that you begin by developing a specific training curriculum (internally or in conjunction with a training organization) that reflects your particular business context. The details of your company's curriculum will depend on your industry, your company's culture, and the expectations of your customer segment.

No matter what your business entails, we encourage you to focus on training employees in how to balance two priorities: the need to provide each customer with anticipatory service and the equally important need to respect the customer's protective bubble. We sometimes refer to this as learning how to be bullish in a china shop. It's hard to quantify this balance; mastering it comes with time and experience. But once it has been achieved, it leads to solid, quantifiable increases in customer loyalty.

Let's examine this balancing act with a practical example that's close to our hearts—our selves as a whole, actually—it surrounds us, in fact. While the two of us work on this book, we're sitting in a fully staffed, comfortable airport club lounge. A few minutes ago, a perfectly nice, well-groomed, well-spoken staff person interrupted Leonardo when he was in mid-sentence. What was lacking here? *Training.* So let's look at how training could effectively apply to this environment.

Otherwise-nice service people obliviously break protective bubbles all the time; training can ensure that *your* employees will do better. Assuming proper selection in the first place for empathy and other necessary traits, proper training can turn the principles below into second nature. Here are the principles we would stress:

Principle 1. Service starts the moment the customer comes in contact with you. The first step of service is a warm and sincere greeting. How do you execute that? At a distance, a guest such as one of us might look up from our work here in the airport lounge, turn, and see an employee coming in from the service door. The employee returns the eye contact and begins service with a sincere smile. The "switch" is turned on; service starts.

But perhaps we didn't actually need anything. The employee needs to continue to maintain eye contact; if it turns out we were just randomly looking up, the employee will recognize that and smile. We would then probably smile back briefly and go back to work. Service has now ended. The employee has reassured us with a smile and should back away, because no service has been requested.

Principle 2: Learn to read the subtle verbal and non-verbal messages the customer is delivering. When customers and guests aren't ready for assistance, they don't like to be disturbed. If they want something, they'll ask. The trick is that the "asking" may be extremely subtle, but employees must be skilled enough to recognize it as clearly as if it had been explicit.

To role-play this principle, we might begin by sitting in the lounge talking with each other; Micah turns his face because he notices peripherally that the employee has walked into the room. The employee makes eye contact and smiles. Micah looks at him, smiles back, and maintains eye contact.

These are sufficient cues: The employee now needs to come a little forward and engage Micah verbally ("Good morning. May I assist you with something?") Why? Because the customer's non-verbal message is "I've seen you; you've smiled at me, and that's super. But I am, by *maintaining* eye contact, trying to bring you closer." (If he didn't need anything, Micah would have concluded the visual exchange as in scenario one: he would have turned right back to talking with Leonardo.)

Principle 3: Adjust to the pace of the customer. You cannot attend to a chatty, meandering tourist in the same way you would serve a time-stressed, introverted banker. It is the server's job to pick up on this.

Principle 4: The bubble is the sanctuary of the guest. If the timing's wrong to disturb the customer, *don't.* Your procedures and timing need to be based on the customer's convenience, not yours. Don't change out the salt and pepper shakers on the table when customers are seated. Don't reach across your customers to light a candle to make the room cozier if the moment's wrong for them, even if it's on your checklist of things to get done. All customer care activity needs to be driven by the *customer's* needs and timing, not ham-fistedly by the employee's rush to check a to-do item off a list. It's simply not service if it doesn't match the customer's timing.

In our lounge example, if the customer opens a little door into his sanctuary and looks up—or makes an obvious break in conversation—*that's* the time to check in. Stay focused enough on your customer that you notice these subtle "door" openings. For example, if Micah and Leonardo have been engaged in constant conversation and then Leonardo turns his head sideways as if looking for somebody, that's the server's chance to step in.

"Yes, sir, how may I assist you?"
"I would like, uh, can you bring another cup of coffee?"
"Absolutely. May I bring a pastry with that also?"
"No, but thanks."

Principle 5: Closing the sanctuary door—or not. When the waiter returns with the coffee, there is a final element. The customer has intentionally come to the foreground with his request for coffee, so the door to his personal sanctuary is now open. The server brings the cup of coffee back, with appropriate niceties. His responsibility now is to ask, *"Is there anything else I can do for you?"*

The customer has two options: "Yes, there is," or "No, there is not." Depending on the answer, the door to the sanctuary may stay open, or it may be shut again. If it's the latter, the server needs to thank the customer graciously and move away.

This is the last principle: the "closing" of service. Too many service interactions end with a cold and impersonal "Bye," or "OK," or nothing at all. The closing of service is as important as the opening. It is the last touch point, and it needs to be handled properly.

Reinforcement: The Daily Check-In

Preparation for serving customers is like a paint job: The thicker and more multi-layered the coating, the more gracefully it will weather. Regardless, over time your employees will suffer wear and tear to their "paint"—from the day-in, day-out strain of working with customers on the one hand and with the demands of management on the other, compounded always by the pressures of life that come from outside work.

This wear and tear can rub even your most naturally friendly employees down to the grain. You need to polish their coats of paint—ideally, every day.

Strangely, the *technical* aspect of a job can actually compound the problem, can actually be part of the grit that chips away every day at the paint of exceptional service. Why? Because service professionals perform the technical parts of their jobs day after day. If someone is a gate agent at Delta or a retail clerk at Bloomingdale's, he will perform the technical aspects of his job daily. He will check people in and out, process transactions, scan items, run credit card payments, day in and day out. And he will end up being very, very good at it.

This, however, is only a portion of his role in the organization: What maintains him in the portion of his role that demands the delivery of caring service—over and over, in a tireless and always subtly different manner? If a company wants to maintain great service, it needs to find a way to discuss service on an ongoing basis and to include everyone from frontline workers on up in the discussions. One way you can do so is with a daily standup meeting.

We know that every industry and every company culture is different. We are far from dogmatic about applying what you could call our daily "standup routine" to every business situation. We have, however, worked in and advised companies that have made revolutionary improvements from implementing this approach. The key is a daily meeting held in small groups throughout your company at the same time each day. Discuss a single aspect of service (for example, one of your guiding service principles, as exemplified by an encounter with a particular customer). Prove your commitment to brevity and focus by holding the meeting standing up, assuming there aren't attendees with physical disabilities who are put at a disadvantage in this setting.

This procedure gets inspiration from, and yet is 180 degrees removed from, the old hospitality tradition of a check-in with staff ("lineup"), where daily specials and other mundane updates are shared. The difference is, in today's world, the challenge of providing great service is not in such nuts and bolts, skills-and-details-related updates. (Put *those* on your wiki.) The challenge is that even if you start off strong with a great orientation, the daily grind will ensure that functional issues ultimately end up overwhelming company purpose.

A daily standup meeting is a chance to keep your company focused on your overriding purpose and to ensure that all staff are aligned to fulfill it. It only takes a few minutes, and the difference it makes can be crucial.

Try it on for size. There is no more powerful way to create an extraordinary experience for your customers than to maintain a fully aligned company—and there is no better time to align a company than once a day, every single day.

CHAPTER EIGHT

Leadership

Guiding the Customer-Centered Organization

Maintaining production capability in a service-oriented business requires a different emphasis than in the world of manufacturing. Your ability to provide service is overwhelmingly are affected by how engaged—how professionally "alive"—the employees are who come in contact with customers. Employee engagement, in turn, is propelled by organizational leadership.

Service Leaders Matter Because People Power Service

On an assembly line, there are traditionally two measures. One measure may be termed "theoretical capacity," the theoretical maximum output of that assembly line during a shift: for example, 100 units. The other counter let's call "forecasted actual production," and also start at an optimistic 100, since nothing generally goes wrong on an assembly line *before* the start of the production day. (Note: This is an admittedly simplified illustration in several respects.) As the day goes on, the units come through the assembly line, until suddenly one unit arrives with a component that won't fit right. This marks the first drop, or "discount," in the "forecasted actual production" number. Ultimately, this second count settles some notches below the ideal 100 by the end of the shift.

By contrast, let's look at the beginning of the shift in a service-focused department. The employees are just showing up. They haven't seen a customer yet. The first employee to arrive is Aviva. On the way back from work yesterday, she had a little car accident. Nothing serious: a little scratch on the door and fender. Unfortunately, this is the new car that she had just picked up on Saturday. Is Aviva upset? Oh, yeah—she's *really* upset.

The second to show up is Mark. How's Mark doing? Well, he just found out that a bill he had overlooked for a couple months is now affecting his ability to buy a house. That stupid $20 medical bill went into collections without him knowing it, and now his credit rating is going to be affected: He's going to be paying $70 to $80 more a month on a thirty-year mortgage. Is he thrown off his game? You'd better believe it.

Do you think that these things don't happen to your employees? They happen all the time—and they downgrade your company's service production capability. Remember: Aviva and Mark *haven't seen a customer yet.* They haven't interacted with another employee. They haven't opened their paychecks to learn that someone in accounting forgot to enter their overtime. But already you're starting with a hobbled organization—in contrast to manufacturing, where production only begins its downward drift once the day has begun.

This is one of the reasons that leadership, starting at the top and spreading throughout the managerial ranks, is so crucial in a service organization. Constant reconnection with workers, as well as constant reconnection of workers with the organization, is your greatest tool. The goal? Having people get to work and think, *"You know what? Maybe if I didn't have to go to work at all it would be better, but since I do have to work, I like this place. It's healthy, clean, supportive, and engaging. So I'm going to give it my attention, performance, commitment, loyalty, and effort."*

Reaching for this state is a central function of a leader in a customer-focused organization.

Five Characteristics of Great Service Leaders

Great service leaders, in our experience, share certain characteristics. The following five are the most crucial for building an exceptional service organization.

1. Vision: The leader is able to dream of the future vividly and then distill that dream into a clear view of where the organization needs to go; to envision, in rich detail, what is to come.

2. Alignment: The successful service leader works to align the entire organization behind a single accessible idea, such as "Customer Focus." Great leaders actively work to simplify complex or abstract ideas into simple, concrete phrases and metaphors that keep people on track. Employees won't always catch implied or obscurely-expressed messages, especially not in diversified, multi-site organizations.

The Cynics Among Us

A leader who assumes the helm in an established organization (or, even more importantly, in a turnaround situation) should address the issue of established cynics and skeptics and their roles in the realignment process. There are at least two possible approaches. One is to terminate the cynics, which is often legally and practically complicated and runs the risk of promoting a new generation of cynics. (*"Do you remember Cheryl in Accounting? She was always saying that management was out to get her. Guess what? They just did . . . I guess they are out to get us!"*)

A more successful approach is to use positive energy and benign neglect to help realign the cranks. Taking this approach, think of your staff in terms of three groups: positive employees, skeptical employees, and cynical employees. Then put nearly all your energy into the positive employees. In such a situation, the true naysayers will tend to quickly move on, and the more moderate "skeptic" sector will fall in line with the positive element that they see receiving your support.

3. Standard Setting: A leader needs to be a manager of processes and a force for performance measurement—there is much more to leadership than just cheerleading. For example, when launching an improvement effort, a leader will not only provide the vision (*"This new packaging initiative is important because it will allow us to become the industry leader in the use of recycled packing materials by the end of next year. And as the recognized leader, we'll have a chance to be an inspiration for many."*). The leader will also insist that appropriate time and other support for the fledgling undertaking are built in to the daily work schedule. Important steps forward need to be given the room they require for proper execution.

A great leader must also be capable of setting performance standards and holding people accountable. Most companies suffer from being inconsistent, which is a by-product of the lack of standards. Without a full complement of well-implemented standards, even the most talented service team will have trouble fighting inconsistency. For example, think about what should be a simple concept: *timeliness*. In traveling the world, you may have noticed how drastically the definition of timeliness varies from culture to culture. If you have teenagers, you've probably noticed that they, too, don't share your standard of timeliness. This is not a complaint against teenagers: They come from a different time-culture than adults, so they have a different understanding of what timeliness implies. But the discrepancy naturally disrupts and demoralizes somebody like you, an ambassador from grown-up culture, when you try to cooperate with your teenagers on an important project. In business, to successfully manage performance you must set, track, and enforce performance standards.

4. *Support:* A good leader won't let an employee suffer with an ineffective toolkit, either literally or figuratively; few things are more demoralizing. Too often, workers are asked to perform their jobs without the proper support. A good leader knows workers need support—specifically, the resources, training, equipment, and material to execute their tasks—and they make sure this support is there.

5. *Motivation, recognition, and reward:* Many leaders underestimate the importance of these factors. Motivation is your employees' flotation device and their swimming coach. When the seas are rough, motivation keeps an employee afloat. It lets her know that she's got support: She can keep swimming and succeed. She can keep going because the goal is up ahead, and she's getting there. At a certain point, she's begun swimming well; she's helping the efforts of the company. You recognize her for the good job she's doing; you give her a prize, a medal, a bonus, or simply a thank you. Great leaders miss few opportunities to recognize somebody for a contribution, and they seek events to celebrate with the same intensity they use to find problems that need to be solved.

Moral Leadership

An employee cannot be treated like a piece of a machine—a cog or a bolt. It's not moral, and it doesn't make business sense: A bolt can't stretch to help a customer. It can only be a bolt. But a person, inspired by a leader, can stretch a bit to the right or left to be helpful—and thus build the value of your business.

What we call the moral leadership of employees involves, at a minimum:

➤ Involving them in the design of the work that will affect them

➤ Enhancing their pride in their work

> Enhancing their purpose, rather than using them only for their function

> Supporting their community and family involvement (however they define "family"), in good times and bad

> Supporting their involvement in areas of the company outside of their strict area of assignment

And, most fundamentally, moral leadership of employees involves knowing that it's wrong to see a worker as "eight hours of labor"— even though, if you look at your Profit & Loss report, labor may be classified as FTEs (full-time equivalents). Companies make hiring requests for shift workers this way, never writing the word *people*: "We need five FTEs, five FTEs insured, three shifts a day, 365 days a year."

People are *not* FTEs.

Leadership Throughout the Ranks

An organization with a great leader will spawn other leaders throughout the ranks. Let's illustrate this in the humblest of settings: The low-level supervisor charged with helping a new worker learn to clean a restroom properly can be a service leader in her own right. How? First, she can convey her vision before any specific skills are taught: Maintaining a clean restroom is the right thing to do, because guests and visitors will appreciate it. When our guests are offered a clean restroom, they'll feel comfortable with our company; they'll look on us with favorable eyes and want to return to our establishment. And return business is very important to our company's financial health.

Then, once she has explained this vision, she'll begin to train her new employee. *("Use these particular chemicals in this particular way, with these particular safety precautions.")* She'll establish and explain the standard for what "cleanliness" means concretely: No trash or dirt on the floor. The mirrors need to sparkle. The trash cans are never more than half full.

A service leader in this position sets up a good measurement and inspection system as well, ensuring that an appropriate level of performance can be maintained on an ongoing basis.

She also makes sure she supports her new worker properly. She supplies him with high quality supplies and ensures that he is trained in their safe and environmentally appropriate usage.

In addition, she communicates frequently and clearly: If the company is expecting an unusual number of visitors on a given day, she lets her employee know in advance.

Finally, she works continually to ensure that her employee is motivated. She lets him know when he is doing a good job and applauds the ways he is helping the organization reach its goal. She involves him in changes to the work processes that affect him, and she looks for opportunities for recognition and advancement for him in the organization.

CHAPTER NINE

What's Worth It, and What's Not?

Pointers on Value, Costs, and Pricing

Customer loyalty is a thing of wonder—and it's a hard-nosed kind of wonder that you can take to your accountant. Loyalty makes customers less price sensitive, more willing to spend money with you, more willing to take a chance on extensions to your product line (assuming you don't abuse this trust in inappropriate ways), and much more immune to competitive entreaties. But no company can afford to spend all of its revenue trying to maximize the customer experience or guarantee customer loyalty. Fortunately, there isn't a need to. In Chapter 6 we explained how systems derived from manufacturing can help service-focused companies minimize their costs behind the scenes. In this chapter, we work through some of our clients' most common concerns about how to control costs while still providing superior service.

What Does Loyalty-Enhancing Service Really Cost?

We would argue that service that wins you loyal customers is well worth it at nearly any cost—because of its immense benefits. Still, what *does* it cost? In some cases, superior service clearly *does* cost more to deliver than average service. For example, the ESF group of summer camps in Pennsylvania and Connecticut employs counselors and staff who are older and more experienced than the "kids counseling kids" you often find in competing institutions. Even the greenest counselor you'll encounter at an ESF camp will be a college student pursuing a degree in early childhood, elementary, or secondary education, child psychology, social work, counseling, or another child-related field. The staff-to-camper ratio is among the lowest in the industry and is cleverly allocated: for example, while one nurse is on premises throughout the day, *two* nurses are put on duty during all peak periods.

Is this approach more expensive than the customary approach? Absolutely. But parents are devoted to the camps; the farthest thing from their minds would be to compare it on a commodity/price point basis with other summer options. Plus, like loyal customers everywhere, *they promote the camps tirelessly to their friends and neighbors.* Recently, in fact, a group of 35 "expat" camp families who had moved from Pennsylvania to Connecticut due to job relocation suggested a new camp location up there to ESF. Even better, they then signed up enough of their New England neighbors and friends to ensure the camps were able to successfully carry off the expansion. (Imagine that: loyal customers who encourage and facilitate your business expansion by serving as your "siting service" and "advance team"—*pro bono.*)

This last point is fundamental: For a fuller accounting of the net cost of maintaining loyalty-building standards such as quality of staffing, you must consider the various kinds of expenses saved and revenue earned through energetic word of mouth marketing, unusually low staff turnover, unusually low client (in this case camper) turnover, lower insurance rates, and elimination or reduction of negligence lawsuits.

Well-trained, well-equipped, and well-treated personnel have longer company tenures, lower accident rates, and fewer behavior problems. When you hire and train the right kind of employees—those who embrace their underlying service purpose in your company—you receive back far more productive work than is achieved by a typical employee in a typical organization. Like the purpose-driven security guard posited in Chapter Seven, patrolling the mall and *also* guiding lost shoppers to their destinations, super-staffers can be—and want to be—everywhere that a customer needs them. They can do this for you, and they *will*. Similarly, solid facilities, high quality tools and materials, strong safety programs, and other key supports for staff and customers: Are they hard to justify sometimes? Hard *not* to justify if you want repeat business—and repeat staff showing up every day and giving you their best performance.

Gilding the Lily

As discussed in Chapter 6 features our customers value need to be shielded from willy-nilly cost cutting. At the same time, there are undoubtedly excesses built into some customer encounters and services. A specific sort of excess you should tune your antennae for is called *lily gilding*. (The term comes from compressing a Shakespeare phrase; the original quote from his *King John* is "To gild refined gold, to paint the lily"—to overdo the already perfect.) Lily gilding is the brilliantly hand-polished finish on an end table—when the end table is always hidden by a tablecloth. It's an air conditioning compressor too powerful for the space it cools.

In customer interactions, lily gilding often takes the form of fancying up your offering beyond what your customers are interested in (or interested in paying for). This has both obvious and hidden costs. The hidden costs include excess features that can make your offering less attractive by complicating it for customers or implying to customers that they're paying for something they don't need.

Finding Gold in De-Gilding

Sometimes, de-gilding will bring a surprise benefit to your customers—and you, in addition to bottom-line savings. In a recent tradition-breaking example, famous glassmaker Riedel realized that the *bowl* was the essence of the wine glass and that the stem, rather than being a necessary feature, was ornamentation that carried drawbacks with it. Mass retailer Target then saw the benefit to themselves in Riedel's new approach, including reduced storage costs and inventory breakage for the retailer, and they brought the product to consumers on a scale that Riedel could never have done by itself. And once a few customers took them home and realized how well they fit into the cupboard and dishwasher and how rarely they broke (having no stem to snap off), they spread the word for free.

"Compared to What?": Value Is Relative

Customers often judge your value relatively. That is, they judge each interaction with your company against their previous interactions with you—and with your competitors. For example, when a passenger gets on an airplane in first class, he expects to be offered his choice of beverage. If he isn't, the service feels wrong. This isn't something each airline can make its own decision about without understanding that its customers' expectations are determined by an *industry-wide standard* for what first-class service means.

To make sure you understand the comparative expectations of your customers, shop the competition—your *best* competition. (Truly shop. Don't just wander in; spend some money, and take a transaction from beginning to end. You may be amazed at what you learn.) Survey the customers of your competition. Survey your *own* customers, or at least customers in your market segment, about the competition. (Do this only anonymously. Never insert questions about the competition into one of your own branded surveys. You damage your brand when, unbidden, you bring up the competition.)

Don't let resentment or insularity lead you to dismiss a competitor's innovations. Think rationally about whether there is value there you could make use of for your own customers.

Pricing Is Part of Your Value Proposition

A good equation for value is "Value = Personal Benefit minus Cost and Inconvenience." But the Personal Benefit variable can easily override the cost factor for a significant sector of the market, at least up to a certain point. Not everybody values money the same, clearly: If commerce were all about low pricing, there would be no space for retailers like Nordstrom; everyone would be shopping at Walmart. Instead, for Nordstrom customers, quality, personal shoppers, and a great return policy provide a Personal Benefit that make the equation—for them—work out in favor of paying more to get more.

Therefore, in product and service design, it helps to focus on the personal benefit you provide for customers in return for the price you charge. In fact, the closer you get to your customer, the more you can minimize price as a consideration—unless, in fact, high price *is* part of the benefit you are providing. (If Tiffany had a "crazy markdown sale" every weekend, would their blue boxes have the same cachet? At Tiffany, the famously high prices themselves confer a benefit to the customer purchasing a gift.)

A loyal customer is the least price-sensitive customer of all. But almost all customers are at least somewhat sensitive to pricing. To unsophisticated customers, a high price is generally a sign of quality. (Homer Simpson never stoops to choosing the *cheapest* wine on the menu; connoisseur that he is, he always picks the *second* cheapest wine on the menu.) But price doesn't always equal quality, and a sophisticated customer often understands this. For example, Costco, a discount chain whose customers skew to well-above-average per capita incomes, has changed the meaning of low prices to "We work hard all the time to find you better value." They stick so consistently with this message that they have elevated it to the level of high theater. On a recent trip there, Micah saw *stamps* discounted at the checkout counter. Costco was apparently happy to lose five cents a roll (not even Costco is able to negotiate with the U.S. Postal Service) to ensure that the very last impression their customers get leaving the store is one of value.

Don't Charge a Customer for Performing the Heimlich

A touchstone in pricing is that your charges should demonstrate that you care about the customer. Goal 1, therefore, is to avoid making customers feel misused—for example, by overcharging them at vulnerable moments. There's a *New Yorker* cartoon we love with two friends walking out of a restaurant. One turns to the other after looking at the check and says, "You're right—they *did* charge you for the Heimlich maneuver." The fact that he *expected* that line item tells you what he thought of the establishment.

Avoid nickel and diming customers by using the rule of thumb that Texas car dealer Carl Sewell made famous long ago: Is this something a friend would charge for? "If you locked yourself out of your car and you called a friend, would he charge you for running a key over?" asked Sewell. "No. Well, we won't either."[1] Ignore Sewell's rule (the way hotels do that not only charge you for long distance calls and bottles of water but do so at rapacious rates) and you'll be tripping yourself up on the path to customer loyalty. Go the extra mile, for free and with a smile, and you'll be helping yourself out as well.

Lots of companies, of course, begin their lives treating customers like friends and avoiding nickel-and-dime insults. But as they evolve, they shift to a different model: They attract customers with a base product that is fairly priced, and then they alienate them with a slew of hidden charges for necessary features. To the extent that you can get away from this model, you will have more loyal customers in the long run. For example, a consultant will do well to look at a project from the viewpoint of the client. A project for an East Coast consulting company quoted as costing $120,000—but requiring that most of the work be done in Seattle—will actually cost significantly more. If the consultant doesn't include the additional, say, $30,000 travel charge in the estimate, the customer is going to feel short-changed when it comes up later. No amount of friendliness will keep them from feeling that you pulled a quick one. You hosed them with a smile—but you still hosed them.

If your pricing policies are not transparent, you also put your workers in a very tight spot defending them. You risk creating angry, distrustful customers *and* a disenchanted work force.

Money Isn't Everything, But Money Issues Matter—Especially How You Present Them

Pricing is a major issue because pricing, like service, is one of the elements of value. It needs to be delivered correctly: Pricing must be presented appropriately, with sensitive language, without surprises, in a way that engenders trust. In this manner, you maintain and grow the value of your service, the trust you have been building with your service, and, ultimately, the loyalty toward which you have been working so hard.

CHAPTER TEN

Building Customer Loyalty Online

Using the Internet's Power to Serve Your Customers and Your Goals

The Internet is the revolutionary structure of our time, not least in its potential to supercharge customer service. This is true for small businesses as well as large now that, as Chris Anderson, editor of *Wired* says, bandwidth, storage, and processing are becoming too cheap to meter.[1]

But don't imagine that the Internet is your guaranteed ally. Many otherwise superb customer-oriented enterprises have marred their reputations by letting the Internet ride *them* instead of saddling its power. How do you harness the power of the Internet to benefit your customers and your business?

The Internet's Double Edge

We recommend focusing on two issues. First, use the Internet correctly and robustly, as expected by your customers. Some of them, after all, are "digital natives," never having known a world without the Web. Such Web-savvy customers expect you to understand the Internet's power and perils just as well as their other favorite companies do. Second, use the Internet's power in a way that celebrates each customer's individuality. Like Luke Skywalker in the presence of the Force, or Bilbo Baggins and his ring, the hidden risk of the Internet's unprecedented capacities is that so much power can pull you toward anticustomer behavior. When the Internet pulls you toward the Dark Side, it will take the discipline and preparation of a Jedi entrepreneur to resist it.

Managing Public Feedback Online

The speed that information travels on the Internet can turn even your "least important" customer into an instant public relations land mine—or gold mine. The phenomenon is different in speed and scope from how brand reputations are made and unmade offline. Online, things can change significantly for your company—positively or negatively—much faster.

Shoe merchant Zappos has benefited from this Internet wildfire. When Zappos offered special return shipping assistance, beyond their company policies, to a woman who couldn't figure out how to handle their standard return shipping procedures in the aftermath of her mother's death, the good word about the company spread quickly throughout the blogosphere.

On the flip side, when a hotel in the Southwest denied Tom Farmer and Shane Atchison hotel rooms at 2 a.m. that they had been guaranteed, they presented their complaint to the hotel as a bitterly funny PowerPoint presentation—and also emailed copies of the presentation to a couple of friends, who then emailed it to a couple of *their* friends, and on and on it spread. Within weeks, the hotel had a public relations fiasco on its hands.

Simple misunderstandings and reasonable differences in viewpoints with customers can become public so quickly on the Internet that you must take measures to anticipate the possibility. We recommend five components to your strategy:

1. *Make yourself unusually easy to reach.* You want your customers to reach out to *you*, not to their blog's readers or their Twitter followers. *You* are who can help them best, and if you help them quickly enough, their frustration is unlikely to be immortalized online.

2. *Respond to public complaints personally, as a human being would.* You'll be amazed how a personal response changes the tenor of an online discussion. After a much publicized, brutally hilarious online skewering of Virgin Atlantic food by a passenger, Richard Branson responded by inviting that passenger to be involved in future menu choices for the airline. Public sentiment turned in Virgin's favor at that point.

We recommend you—or an executive at your company who is terrific at such things—get in there online and let your complainant know that you care, you're paying attention, and you're glad to clarify and assist. (Set up a Google Alert [www.google.com/alerts] for your company and for your product name, including any likely misspellings, so you will be notified immediately upon such postings.) The complainant may alter the original posting if convinced by you that it's unfair—if this is done quickly enough, there's a chance the original version of the posting won't even get indexed. If not, we still recommend you get into the discussion. Place contrite, explanatory comments on the site if it accepts comments. Come across as a real person—a very, very nice one—and most discussion participants will treat you like one.

3. *Control who in your company responds—and who doesn't.* When an Internet PR crisis emerges, you need a lockdown mentality, so that one "designated driver" can handle it. The first employee who notices the crisis should alert the designated driver, and nobody else should respond unless so instructed, to avoid unauthorized and potentially inflammatory or contradictory responses.

4. *Be careful not to be too "clever" online—it may not turn out how you'd like.* There is a specific cyber term for disguised online

cleverness, like posing as someone you're not in order to goad the competition: *trolling*. Avoid being branded as a troll.

5. *Use your evangelists—but with care.* If you have loyal customers, then you have at least a few precious *evangelists*: people who want to stick up for you and spread the word. If you feel comfortable imposing on some of them, you can ask them to stick up for you online with a few well-placed *"I'm sorry you experienced that; I've never had anything like that happen to me. Perhaps it was a misunderstanding."* You don't want to pile it on and, again, these need to be sincere, credible postings by real customers who are willing to identify themselves online—not staffers posing as customers. (See trolls, above.)

Opinions: Everybody Has One. Evangelists: Every Company Needs Them

Last year on a short-lived reality television show, the great British restaurateur Marco Pierre White tricked his apprentices into single-mindedly sucking up to a mystery "food critic"—and then scolded them for doing so. In fact, there was no single critic at the restaurant. Chef White had given *each* of the customers that night a Zagat-style rating card to fill out. Our opinion? He was preparing his apprentices for the Internet age by doing so. While even a few years ago, people might find their best hope of generating buzz in gaining the ear of one well-placed critic, someone like a *New York Times* reviewer, a *Today Show* correspondent, or a talk show host, nowadays, in most markets, the road to success is to strive to please *every* critic—which is to say, every customer—rather than one elite keeper of the key. And to do so before the winds shift against you online.

On the other hand, building evangelists for your company is as important as ever. "[Your article] did a disservice to composers and players," began a response recently in one of the largest forums covering the sector of the entertainment industry[2] in which Micah's company, Oasis, operates. What was the "disservice"? The article had dared to positively mention one of Oasis' competitors—while neglecting to mention Oasis in the article. This unsolicited letter was the kind of publicity that every company yearns for, so Micah looked back to see how they had created such an evangelist. The source? A veteran saleswoman at Oasis, in no fewer than 20 back-and-forth online exchanges over a period of weeks, had taken it upon herself to patiently answer each question this gentleman had posed, having no idea the dividend it would ultimately pay.

The Internet Can Promote Commoditization. Avoid This Through Individualization

Use the incredible distributed power of the Internet, but balance it with individualization. For a simple example, consider the standard way that online FAQs (Frequently Asked Question lists) conclude by asking, *"Did this answer your question?"* For the most part, this approach works: You've served many customers with a single response, your customers have avoided waiting in a queue, and you get to ask each of these customers whether your answer was effective, so you can refine it for the future.

What's not to like? Nothing—*if* you go the extra step of individualizing this feature of your website. You need to have a way to identify and reach out to the frustrated customers who answered "No" to the concluding question. (Remember, *"No"* here means the question wasn't answered, so it should be read as meaning *"Heck no!—Help!"*). That way you can get back to them in some fast, effective, individualized way that says, "We care that this didn't work for you!"

To build loyalty, build this kind of individualized content into each online service feature.

Long Copy/Short Copy

One way the Internet helps address your customers' individuality is by allowing them to choose between "long copy" (in which you spell out all the fascinating/grueling details) and "short copy" (the short, snappy advertisement-like summary version). Since you can't know which version a particular customer wants, provide both and let them choose.

To quote Mark Penn (the formidable pollster known best for identifying the emergence of the "soccer mom" demographic trend) on the subject:

> Be careful before you accept the conventional wisdom that Americans can't concentrate, that we are too distractible for sustained narrative, and that political office always goes to the candidate with the cleverest tag line. In fact, a sizable number of us—often the most interested key decision makers—will listen for as long as you can talk, read for as long as you can write, and follow for as long as you are willing to explain something.[3]

Like Penn, you may have noticed a diversity of reading styles and attention spans among your customers. With the capabilities of the Web, you no longer need to impose a single writing style on, or suppose a single reading style for, all of your customers. You can let different customers choose what works for them. The "short copy" will, of course, be what you put up front: a brief product or service description and pricing. As this may be all that many customers need, they won't be slowed down by any minutiae. Other customers can click on a "learn more" button for a few paragraphs of additional insight. But don't necessarily stop there: Why not include "white papers" or other background material you have available for those customers or prospects who want to do more thorough research on your offering? On the Web, with good design these additional resources do not need to add significantly to the clutter of your layout.

Online, the Window in Which to Show You're Extraordinary Can Be Small

The Internet makes it relatively easy for companies with no tradition of good service to provide at least *tolerable* service—by buying or building a highly usable web interface and battle-testing it regularly. While this is good for consumers, it presents a dilemma for us: If tolerable self-service is becoming widely available, how do we distinguish ourselves online?

In large part, by augmenting technology with direct, loyalty-building care and attention.

The Finishing Touch for "Perfect" Websites: Human Contact

Netflix, as we touched on in Chapter Six, boasts a superbly designed online self-service system that makes "perfect purchasing"—lending, actually—possible, generally without any human interaction at all. Nonetheless, the bottom line is that in a competitive market in which perfect products are emerging all around you, it's not enough to offer a perfect online experience. To develop customer loyalty, you must *also* provide outstanding human-to-human touch points, whenever they may be called for.

To this end, Netflix not too long ago decided to buck the trend of trying to minimize service costs: It actually set for itself the goal of providing far more human-to-human contact, any time a customer seemed to be looking for it, than its competitors do. They did away with Internet-based customer service responses altogether, instead displaying their 1–800 service number prominently on their site, and they refused to farm out any of those telephone service jobs to subcontractors overseas. Rather, they built a massive new telephone customer service center in the greater Portland, Oregon, area. Portland was picked specifically as a trait-based hiring move: In encounters with the existing Portland work force, Netflix executives had discovered an unusually high proportion of people with great customer service traits such as "politeness and empathy"[4] already located there.

Search for automated and human-powered ways to provide personal attention to your most needy online customers:

1. *Encourage personal interactions at every juncture for customers who may desire them—no matter how "perfect" your site seems without them.* Provide live chat buttons on every page. Post your toll-free service number prominently, and keep the line open as far into the night as you can effectively staff it. Provide an "urgent email" button. (As we've mentioned, some people prefer to correspond by email, and for people with disabilities it is often the best option.)

2. *Design the elements of your site with sensitivity, so you don't exclude any of your customers.* Customers with disabilities, ranging from subtle to daunting, are at least as active online as they are in the physical world. There are specific ways to make your site more widely usable to these customers that you should be sure to follow. For example, each fancy graphic element on your site should have an "alt" tag (similar to a caption) that can be read by a text reader, so that you can serve customers with visual impairments. More broadly, older customers are rapidly becoming more comfortable online, and yet many sites look like they're still being designed exclusively for twenty-somethings, with tiny buttons and confusing layouts. If there's somewhere you want someone to click, make it obvious. This is the Internet version of being sensitive to the "pace" of your customers.

3. *Make the self-service elements of your site fun and interesting.* Self service can be engaging too. Think about comedian Demetri Martin's idea for a coin change-making machine that behaves like a slot machine: Bells ring and lights flash, just as though you've struck the jackpot—even though you still get back the same amount of money you put in. Incorporate that vision into how you think about designing self service, and you'll never think it has to be a dull experience for your customers again.

4. *Make any automated correspondence you use more engaging, personable, and, if appropriate, funny.* If you use automated follow-up emails, consider a lighthearted approach, perhaps like the follow-ups Micah resorted to during understaffed periods in the early years:

Hi! This is your friendly robotic follow up (sorry about that,
but almost everything else *about Oasis is 100 percent per-*
sonal, so if you hit "reply", you'll get a real human being im-
mediately, so you can bond with someone of your own
species.) . . .

CD Baby, a sister company to Oasis, uses even the smallest of opportunities to show how personable they are: They turned the email
confirmation that lets you know a CD has shipped into friendly, campy
comedy. Their whimsical email helps buyers realize that this company
is different—that it's staffed by people whose priority is being creative,
joyful human beings just like themselves:

Your CDs have been gently taken from our CD Baby shelves
with sterilized contamination-free gloves and placed onto a
satin pillow. A team of 50 employees inspected your CDs
and polished them to make sure they were in the best possi-
ble condition before mailing. Our packing specialist from
Japan lit a candle and a hush fell over the crowd as he put
your CDs into the finest gold-lined box that money can buy.
We all had a wonderful celebration afterwards and the whole
party marched down the street to the post office, where the
entire town of Portland waved "Bon Voyage!" to your pack-
age, on its way to you, in our private CD Baby jet on this day,
Monday, April 6th![5]

"I made no haste in my work," declared Thoreau in *Walden*, "but
rather made the most of it."[6] Haste seemed like a clear negative in
Thoreau's world. But what about in ours? In a sense, our customers
want us to make haste: They want us to generate great results with a
minimum of their time and effort. Meanwhile, we strive to bind our
customers to our brands—largely by making the very most of each en-

counter with them. We need to lavish time and attention on them to help the attachment process along. To reconcile these goals, do what CD Baby has done with a simple shipping alert: Design each online step to get the most positive human connection out of it that you can—without slowing down or inconveniencing your customers.

Online, the Golden Rule Is *Permission*

For a decade, Seth Godin has been drawing attention to the concept of "permission marketing," which he defines as the privilege of delivering *anticipated, personal, relevant messages to people who actually want to get them*. Seth emphasizes that treating people respectfully is the best way to earn their attention. In his worldview, when people choose to *pay* attention, they actually are paying you—giving something valuable to you. Once they've spent some amount of attention on you, it's lost to them forever. So Seth emphasizes that we must think about a customer's attention as an important asset—something to be respected and valued by us, not wasted. Meaningful permission is different from technical or legal permission:

> *Just because you somehow get my email address doesn't mean you have permission. Just because I don't complain doesn't mean you have permission. Just because it's in the fine print of your privacy policy doesn't mean it's permission either. Real permission works like this: If you stop [contacting them], people complain, they ask where you went.*[7]

Jonathan Coulton, an Internet indie-music phenomenon, can email nearly any customer who buys one of his CDs or MP3 downloads online and have them be happy to hear from him. Coulton has real *permission* to contact his fans—they *want* to hear from him. But what if your company sells someone a replacement cell phone charger through Amazon Marketplace? It's a lot touchier: Odds are good your customers are not obsessive cell phone charger fans. You almost certainly don't have their real permission to flood their in-boxes. Your messages are unlikely to be anticipated, personal, or relevant.

Amazon.com: A Brilliant Company, but Not the Most Realistic Model to Emulate

In online commerce, there's Amazon.com and then there's everyone else.

Amazon's astonishing ability to create loyal customers is a wonderful and enviable thing to behold—but it's not a directly replicable model for the rest of us in business. Amazon's success is based at least in part on a much riskier and more expensive approach to loyalty than our anticipatory service model: an incredibly well executed version of the *repetition* strategy. Get the basics of satisfactory service exactly right and then repeat the customer's exposure until loyalty occurs. The repetitions in Amazon's case come fast and furious, because their perfect product eliminates friction like nobody else can.

Here are just a very few examples of Amazon's friction-free service:

➤ Your credit card is stored in its entirety for your convenience. (In fact, if you ever need to register a new credit card, Amazon doesn't even make you *flip the card over* to find and input the security code.) What's more, you can choose "one click" purchasing and make an entire purchase without re-entering, re-selecting, or re-considering anything: type of payment, delivery address, billing address, or method of shipment. All in all, there is almost nothing payment-wise to interfere between your brain desiring to make a purchase and your ability to instantly do so.

➤ Your order is transmitted instantly to the shipper, often UPS in Lexington, Kentucky. This makes it possible to order well into the evening and—in a pinch—receive that item early the next morning with nearly 100 percent accuracy.

➤ Amazon can help direct you to precisely the right product for you, thanks to its unparalleled use of the power of customer rankings from its millions of customers.

Amazon has a unique combination of attributes that are probably not realistic goals for most of us: being first; being huge; having abnormally deep pockets. For example, Amazon's packages can be transported to customers more quickly and cheaply than competitors' products because leading carriers will agree to almost anything to get Amazon's *extraordinarily* high-volume shipping contracts. Furthermore, Amazon's near-monopoly gives it the freedom to let customers post critical comments about merchants' products without losing any good merchants (for good merchants, it's much more profitable to stay on Amazon and take their critical lumps on a few products). To create a friction-free payment and account experience, Amazon had to spend unknown amounts of money developing extremely strong, often proprietary, and always obsessively enforced security strategies (their Chief Technology Officer hints that Amazon makes internal use of "a group of hackers whose goal in life it is to break into"[8] their system, thus proving its strength). It's only through the very expensive efforts of some of the top programmers and security experts in the world that Amazon has been able to deliver a friction-free Web experience *and* deliver extreme account security.

Amazon is also powerful enough and perfect enough to deemphasize human-to-human customer service on a day to day basis. In a crisis you may be able to reach a fantastic employee at Amazon (we absolutely have), but it's just as likely that you will be affronted by someone with limited people skills deploying a form letter when you're frustrated and irate (that's happened to us, too, more than once). You may get away with that for a while, probably a long while, if you're a near-monopoly delivering the most perfect product in the world. But all others—the rest of us—need to strive instead for a consistently superb human touch.

While there's always something to learn from this brilliant merchant, (including how to build a truly "perfect product" and how to keep up and keep improving upon such a high standard for self service), overall Amazon.com is not the most realistic model for most of us. In most industries, it's not realistic to aspire to a catalog as extensive as Amazon's or an online experience that is as friction-free. (Or to working on such a scale: We'll wager you're not going to be selling and shipping a reputed 2.5 Nintendo Wiis *per minute*.)[9]

So we expect your path to loyalty online will be different from Amazon's. Aim for perfection on a smaller scale—imbued with caring at each of many human touch points.

First Time Online: A Nuts-and-Bolts Case Study

Suppose you have a traditional brick-and-mortar business, and you want to add an Internet presence for the first time. How should you go about it, step by step? We find it helpful to work with each of our brick-and-mortar clients individually, when establishing them online. But many of the principles we apply with them are universal. To illustrate, let's consider a semi-hypothetical rug cleaning business, one that has never before ventured online.

First, why go online? Well, a lot of homeowners now prefer to begin researching topics like rug cleaning online. (How often is it needed? How common are overcharges and scams? How much does it cost?) So before using the Yellow Pages, they venture onto the Web and search for "rug cleaning."

An approach you might consider to attracting business is well removed from starting with a hard sell. Rather, it's providing reliable, free information. Think about it: As an expert in the business for multiple years, you've got to know pretty much everything there is to know about rug cleaning. Your opinions are valuable. Why not become the online go-to source for free, expert advice on rug cleaning? Give away this information and revenue will come back to you—in the form of customers who stumbled across you even before they thought they were searching for your service.

There are many ways to create an online informational presence (YouTube videos; guest blogging; an information-only area of your commercial website interwoven with links to your services and products; etc.). Being the go-to place for free information online is terrific. It magnifies your perceived trustworthiness. It appeals to potential customers, because giving away expert information makes you an expert—their expert. And it brings potential customers to your virtual doorstep.

Just be careful not to make these same offerings into explicit advertisements for your own product. Consumers often prefer to have a feeling of separation between their information-gathering sessions and their service-selection sessions online. (Don't make the converse mistake either of making it unclear that you're open for business should homeowners be looking. Just keep that information segregated tastefully.)

What should your business's own *commercial* website look like? Overall, your site should feature friendly introductory information highlighting what's better about your approach, your technology, your background, your people—whatever is important to your prospective customers. Base your approach on the long copy/short copy model: Keep it brief up front, but make additional information accessible as desired for those who want more.

Next, use the power of computer-driven modeling to make it easy for your visitors to compute a realistic estimate of the cost of your services. They should be able to enter the basics (X number of rooms, X number of flights of stairs, entry hall or no entry hall) and immediately receive a clear and thorough report.

To make your site feel welcoming, customers should be able to use such features *without* entering their password, geographic location, or other personal information. Once customers are accustomed to the site and using it appreciatively, *then* offer a chance to password-protect, store, and annotate their sessions. Give them a chance to buy *themselves* in to your company.

Less Can Be More with Preconfigured Software "Solutions"

If you buy powerful Web technology preconfigured by a specialized software company in your industry, your best service outcomes may result from *turning off* features that make things difficult for the customer, like requirements to immediately log in with a password, and other similar stumbling blocks for prospects when you are just "meeting and greeting" each other.

Let a customer who wants to be contacted choose her contact time and submit it on a Web form. Monitor the workings of this form on a regular basis (make sure your methods of monitoring include our recommended [Chapter 3] idiot-proof method—i.e., try it yourself) to ensure that the form gets to your scheduling department.

Now, finally, comes the first human touch point. Here is your chance to start building loyalty. Call at the appointed time. And have your nicest of nice, best trained person do the calling: someone sensitive to the fact that the person being called may not even immediately recall having made this "appointment," multitaskers that we all are. You need someone with impeccable telephone manners. Someone sensitive to the resistance that any business phone call, even a previously requested one, may elicit at home. Her call should sound approximately as follows: *"Good morning, this is Mary from Fuzzy Rug Cleaning. I received a request to call this morning, to speak with Ms. Sinclair. Is she available?"*

The next human touch point will be when your cleaning technician arrives at the Sinclair residence. Have the *same* nicer-than-nice employee call to confirm the appointment:

Hello, Ms. Sinclair. Good morning. I'm calling again from Fuzzy Rug. This is just a courtesy call. I want to reconfirm that

our technician will arrive at your house between 5:00 and
7:00.

Think how refreshing this Internet-originated experience has been. Without intrusion, without inconvenience, a customer has found the information she needed: specific, personalized, customized information. She has decided for herself how much personal information to reveal. She has used Internet scheduling to ask a company to work on *her* schedule—not to conform to theirs. And when the time came, a warm person, with impeccable telephone manners, moved the exchange gracefully into the human dimension.

Let's assume that your technician arrives on time and does an excellent job. And that your billing is fair and handled effectively, with a thoughtful thank you and farewell given at the end of the project. At this point, you have made excellent strides toward winning a powerful ally for your company—someone who will be a loyal repeat customer and also recommend you to her friends. You've done this by harnessing the power of the Internet to draw her near to you—and by using the power of skilled and caring personal contact to keep her close.

CHAPTER ELEVEN

Hello/Good-Bye

Two Crucial Moments with a Customer

We've been tough taskmasters throughout this book, urging you to do everything right and to never let up. We've drilled in the value of putting in exceptional effort, day and night, with your customers. But there is a place for shortcuts in customer service, too. In Chapter 3, we mentioned that concentrating on certain *crucial emotional moments* with your customers is your guarantee that you're putting your efforts where they make the most difference—where they lodge most vividly in memory. We covered one of these crucial emotional moments, *service recovery,* in Chapter Four. Now we focus on the other two: *hello* (your greeting) and *good-bye* (your farewell).

Hellos and good-byes are beginning and end points, the two highest positions in what memory researchers call the *serial position curve.* In a list of items or events, they will be remembered most easily. If you want to prove this to yourself, follow in the footsteps of memory researcher Elizabeth Loftus and give a friend a list of items to remember—let's say turkey, salt, pepper, tomatoes, pumpkin, cheese, milk, oregano, chili powder, butter. Odds are good that the first and last items (turkey and butter) will be the ones most easily remembered [1].

The same is true for hellos and good-byes. Handle them superbly, and you'll reap a disproportionate dividend in what "sticks" as a customer's opinion of you.

Timelessly Time-Sensitive

Greetings and first impressions have been uniquely important to human relationships for thousands of years. Odysseus's son Telemachus knew that first impressions matter: "[H]e glimpsed Athena now and straight to the porch he went, mortified that a guest might still be standing at the doors," writes Homer.[2]

Fast-forward a few millennia to postcard-perfect Bar Harbor, Maine, where Chris Cambridge owns The Scrimshaw Workshop, a gift shop perched next door to an immensely popular ice cream shop. Chris understands the importance of a good "hello" as well as the ancient Greeks: While customers at other shops are greeted with a "No Food, No Drink" sign, or, at best, "Please Finish Your Food or Drink Before Entering Our Store," Chris bucks this trend. Imagine how many more customers Chris wins by upending this norm with this welcoming (and brave) statement:

YES! YOU MAY BRING IN YOUR ICE CREAM CONES
—Just be careful of their drips.

To make *sure* you get the idea that his store is a welcoming place, Chris added this in a smaller font:

P.S. We love your dogs, too!

(See the sign at www.micahsolomon.com)

In many businesses, it's a front desk receptionist, host, or other human greeter who welcomes and bids farewell to visitors. So, it's crucial that the person in this position conveys a warm welcome and a gracious, heartfelt farewell; the handling of these two moments is key to your brand's image. This is why inbound and outbound reception is best handled by a skilled, trained, and motivated veteran with great customer-focused traits. It's why we recommend against treating reception as an entry-level, stepping-stone position—because, whatever you call it, "First and Last Impression Creator" is among the most important positions in your enterprise.

Which Level of Service Do You Provide? Let Them Know from "Hello"

One of the first things a greeting does is convey the level of service a customer may expect from your establishment. Are they going to get *non-compliant* service, *compliant* (reactive) service, or *anticipatory* service?

Non-compliant service ("Can I get some water from you, please?" *"Uh, there's a vending machine down the street."*) will push away customers every time. They asked for a glass of water and received nothing—except a grudging set of directions. (In fact, non-compliance is such a wretched level of "service" that we've given our readers the respect of wasting very little copy on it in this book.)

Compliant service ("May I have some water?" *"Certainly. Here you go!"*) is pretty much the baseline for the contemporary business world. It doesn't offend customers, but it won't win them over either. Compliant service can be well-executed, but it's not going to build loyalty for your brand.

Anticipatory service (*"Welcome. It is such a hot day today. May I offer you a glass of water?"*) is extremely rare. But as we've discussed, this is where customer loyalty is created. When customers' wishes are anticipated, they get to bask in the magical feeling of being cared for. That feeling creates loyalty, which builds strategic value for your company.

So, if you can tip your hand at the front door that this exceptional level of service is what they can expect—if you can manage to literally "have them at hello"—you will predispose your customers to think well of you throughout the rest of the service experience.

Greeted properly and warmly, a customer will be less sensitive to minor issues later in the encounter. A good greeting enhances subsequent human interactions and can—significantly—affect a customer's perception of a physical product that is offered for sale.

A crucial aspect of a proper greeting is recognition. What is recognition? Being seen, literally and figuratively: being acknowledged, being welcomed, and being appreciated. Recognition, to cite Danny Meyer again, is "the number one reason guests cite for wanting to return."[3]

When a customer is arriving on a *repeat* visit, this should be a special type of recognition: that the customer was *missed,* that his return fills a gap that was there in his absence. Beth Krick, an administrator we admire at a small primary school in Pennsylvania, greets the children and parents every morning at drop-off. So, when a child or a parent is absent for a few days, Ms. Krick is sure to notice, and she commemorates the return with a heartfelt *"We missed you."* What a standard for any company, of any size, in any field, to strive for: to give that level of simple recognition to every returning customer.

The Customer May Come in Contact with You Earlier Than You Expect

Remember that service begins as soon as the customer comes in contact with you—but only the *customer* gets to determine when that first moment is, and it may be much earlier than you think, or would wish. For example, suppose a customer parks his car in a retailer's parking lot, and the first things he sees are broken chain link fencing and cigarette butts strewn all about. In this instance, the first contact has occurred, unbeknownst to the retailer, who now must struggle to overcome this negative impression. It's unfair (the retailer may not even control the lot), but it's reality. This is why every carefully managed resort pays attention to the arrival sequence: the flowers, the signage, the friendly security guard at the gatehouse, the doorman. By the time you get to your room, you should feel gently transported to another world.

Don't Rush Your Hellos and Good-Byes on the Telephone

A proper telephone answering sequence includes an *appreciative greeting*, a *clear introduction*, and a *sincere offer of assistance*. Calls are closed with a *personalized farewell* and a *warm invitation to return*. In many companies, the opening can be short, but still sweet: *"Thank you for calling L&M Stagers! This is Bill. How may I help you?"* (But not: *"L&M Stagers! This is Bill."*) The closing can be as simple as *"Thank you for calling, Mrs. Peterson. I hope your project works out well for you and that you'll think of us the next time you're in town."*

It's easy to imagine that it takes too long to handle hellos and good-byes properly. But actually, a whopping six extra seconds per call is sufficient to answer *and* close the call this way. If you get thirty calls a day you would be investing a full three minutes per day in delivering excellent customer service that will impress the callers—three minutes in the course of an eight-hour work day! So don't let volume become an excuse for slipshod hellos and good-byes on the telephone.

Serving Disabled Customers Is a Responsibility *and* an Opportunity, from the Moment You Welcome Them at Your Door

Your facility's entrance—your visual "hello"—is where your attitude toward customers with disabilities is most clearly on display. We understand how in some business settings, after years with nobody in a wheel-chair showing up, keeping your ramps clear and in top condition may seem like a service to . . . exactly nobody. But we don't think of it that way. Instead, we remember that visibly inviting and welcoming disabled clients sends a powerful message not only to them, but to their families, friends, and the myriad others who care about them. It says that you have broken down barriers to entry; you're on the right side of this issue.

Did you know that the majority of physically challenged customers do not use wheelchairs or scooters? It's important for you as a business leader to understand the full range of physical disabilities and to become aware of cost-effective ways to make your establishment more compatible with them. Many disabilities are subtle, and you will only understand how to accommodate them if you spend some time studying them. For example, in our aging society a very common disability is arthritis and related (and often very painful) musculoskeletal disorders. This is a good reason to use "universal access" handles instead of round doorknobs at all of your points of entry, on restroom facilities, and wherever else possible within your facility. It's also an important reason to make doors self-closing and only lightly weighted. It is a good investment to read some of the best source books on this subject. Directly or indirectly, thousands of dollars have likely been spent—or should be spent—making the "bones" of your facility appropriate for disabled customers; your research will ensure that investment is used appropriately.

Visual and auditory disabilities are also quite common. Make sure you're creating an unusually positive "greeting" for such customers and their allies, in person and online.

The web has huge potential as an equalizer for people with sight and hearing loss. As a first step, make sure you aren't inadvertently slamming a virtual door in their faces in any of these common ways:

> *Captchas.* These are letters and/or numbers rendered as an image rather than text, in order to require a real human being to look at the

screen. By thus separating human and automated input, a captcha can help achieve the very admirable goal of preventing automated hacker attacks. The problem: Captchas are also unreadable by a visually impaired person who uses a screen text reader. This undoes decades of progress in accessibility; if you don't have a legitimate need to use captchas on your site, *don't*. If you do, find a captcha program with an *intelligible* audio alternative.

➤ *Graphics without readable alt tags.* An alt (alternate) tag, as we've mentioned, describes or substitutes for the image when using a text reader. Think of it as a caption. Make sure your web team checks the comprehensiveness and accuracy of your alt tags just as carefully as you proofread your site for, say, dead links.

➤ *No way to get service except by phone.* If a customer who is hearing impaired wants to contact you to return an item, is email offered as an alternative? If telephone-only is your policy (because you're trying to re-sell them or for some other reason), then you'd better have a well-functioning TTD/TTY machine to support special-needs customers. But we recommend including email support for them as well.

Of course, barriers to entry can occur at many places other than entry and exit points. For someone using a wheelchair, a single narrow hallway with no reasonable and clearly marked alternate route can botch the whole deal. Here are some other bottlenecks we've seen that shout "I don't care much about you!"

➤ The celebrated spa that always has a fresh floral arrangement perched on (and thus blocking the use of) the toilet stall's grab bar

➤ The lavishly renovated espresso cafe—with a juice cooler jutting out to make the turn into the restroom impossible in a wheelchair

➤ The railing for a bustling National Park Service gift shop's ramp that is entirely obscured by overflow merchandise

> The office building elevators that have the slot for keycard access placed high above the buttons

> The many businesses that put their vehicles and dumpsters in the cross-hatched areas next to handicapped spaces, apparently unaware that this area is necessary for wheelchair and scooter loading and unloading

> *(Photographic food for thought at micahsolomon.com)*

In addition to the physical aspects of your product, it is important to consider the way your staff interacts with the physically challenged guests they are assisting. Too often we see service workers towering over a guest in a wheelchair or grabbing a visually impaired guest by the arm in an attempt to guide her somewhere (rather than offering an arm for the guest to take). There are plenty of good training programs on the market for how to properly serve disabled customers. It is well worth investing in one.

Turn Your Receptionist into a Predator (Who Kills with Kindness)

It's okay to be a bit goofy when you're training your staff: A bit of over-the-top oratory is one of the best ways to make things memorable. For example, here's a metaphor that Leonardo offers as a silly, imaginative, exaggerated way to explain the job of a greeter:

> *A predator cat loiters, prowls, watches, and waits. Then as soon as something enters its hunting ground, the cat is suddenly hyper-alert, intently focused: Am I going to hunt this? To serve our customers, think and act like that cat. Become as alert as the predator cat does when prey enters its territory. And focus single-mindedly on deciding: Is service called for in this situation?*
>
> *Your hunting ground is the reception area: It starts at the*

front door, and extends to the elevator lobby. No customers should ever pass by your area without you focusing on them and being ready to "hunt" them. How many times have you yourself stepped into a building and the receptionist is behind the counter doing her thing, and you have to get to the counter to trigger her attention? That receptionist isn't acting like a top predator.

If she were, then whenever someone crosses her hunting ground, her instinct would be to scan the area immediately in order to figure out what the movement is. And if it's the right moment, she would move in to see whether there is something she can pounce on—I mean, someone who needs assistance!

Goofy? Sure. But a dollop of goofiness enlivens the training process. And it adds considerable spark to the daily routine of your receptionists to have a picture in their minds of themselves as predators, with everyone who passes through the reception area evaluated as potential prey.

It's Google—Not You—Who Decides Where Visitors Enter Your Site. Be Sure They're Greeted Properly Anyway

Here's an online conundrum: "Hello" is crucial—but *you* can't decide which page on your site your visitors first land on. *Google* is in charge of where most of your visitors will land. And, of course, Murphy's Law will ensure that they land on some arcane, highly technical back corner of your website—one that definitely doesn't put your best foot forward!

Let's outwit Murphy with this three-pronged strategy:

1. Anticipate that "lost" visitors will arrive (via Google, links embedded in Wikipedia, etc.) on obscure inner pages of your site, and respond by making *each* page extremely welcoming. Include:

➤ The name of the proprietor (and often a portrait with some words of welcome)

➤ A live chat link

➤ A "first time here?" tour button

➤ A "contact me now" button

2. Consider *paying* to reduce the wrong points of entry. There are various ways to persuade people to come in through the front door, as it were. You can use Google Adwords and other pay-per-click options, such as banner advertising on the favorite sites of your prospective customers. Placing your bait carefully in the online waters where the customers you want are swimming is, in many cases, a notable improvement over inefficient "spray and pray" advertisements on television, radio, and general-interest printed matter.

One of the features of targeted online advertising is your ability to control prospective new customers' points of entry. People who click on such ads can be directed to an inviting and uncluttered page, where you provide the most relevant initial meet-and-greet information. You can even ask for their permission to market to them—in effect, to begin a dialogue with them about their needs and your services. Of course, ask them for the *minimum* information possible. If you can get the first part of your message across by email, then just ask for a first name and an email address. As always, offer them an easy out. If they want to get to your regular site, make it clear how to do so. If they want to chat or email with you, put those links on this page as well.

3. For visitors who arrive directly at your homepage, provide different experiences for new (unrecognized) visitors than for returning customers—just as you would in the physical world. For returning visitors, welcome them back and invite them to personalize the visit. For new visitors (or ones you can't recognize), welcome them with a "new here?" screen and invite them to start a dialogue with you: take a guided tour, receive some free information—anything to keep them from wandering off before you have some way to keep in touch.

Taking Control of Good-Byes

Good-byes are often rushed—or skipped altogether. After all, you are frequently so relieved to have gotten one job wrapped up successfully, and to be able to move on to the next one. So a transaction often ends with an invoice. What a wasted opportunity! If your customers are happy, the good-bye is your last, and one of your most notable, chances to bond with them, to add an important final chapter to the service story.

Try to close each interaction with your customer in a way that is memorable and sincere. Too many otherwise-fine service experiences come to a miserable close that consists solely of handing back a credit card or "OK" or "NEXT." How much hard-earned good will is lost that way? A *lot*.

So, try to never close an interaction without providing a personalized farewell and an invitation to return. If handled properly, this farewell will be *personal*, *resonant*, and *long lasting* (see below)—but before you move to the closing, make sure you ask a final question, slowly and sincerely: *"Is there anything else I can do for you?"* If the answer is "No, thank you," then move to the closing, as follows:

1. *Personalize it:* Use the customer's name, for starters. Offer your business card, if appropriate for your type of business. Beyond these obvious things, *customize* your language to fit this customer's history with you. For example, if this is the last day of a convention or holiday, add your sincere wishes for safe travel. If you are a retailer, express your hope for satisfaction with the item purchased.

2. *Make it resonant:* If appropriate, give a parting gift. It can be a lollipop for the customer's child, a vintage postcard, or a book. An ideal gift is something that is emotionally resonant with your brand as well as appropriate to the customer. *Invite your customer to come back again as she leaves.*

6. *Long lasting:* Unless inappropriate for the type of purchase, send a follow-up note. Personal and handwritten is better than preprinted—this is the best $1 investment you may ever make.

A Good-Bye Gaffe

Your good-bye at the end of successfully resolving a customer's trouble call should never morph into an attempt to make an additional sale. Trouble calls need to be about just one thing: solving the customer's problem. Customers feel especially vulnerable and dependent on you during these calls, because you're the only one who can help them. Since they feel one down, for you to sneak in a sales pitch at the last moment can come across as having their arms twisted or being bait-and-switched. Yes, they may buy whatever you're pitching at that moment, but they'll often resent you for it later.

The Hazards of Subcontracting Your Hellos and Good-Byes

Be cautious about subcontracting your greetings and your farewells. Of course, subcontracting is often a necessary part of business; properly handled, it can be appropriate and desirable. But such arrangements can also be Trojan Horses, filled with enemies of your cause who ransack the precious goodwill of your customers—sometimes even before the customers quite make it in the door.

We're being melodramatic in our language about this to make sure you mark our words with special care: The quality of the subcontractor's entire staff, their selection process, their training standards, their appearance and grooming, their code of conduct—*everything*—has to be absolutely integrated with your own. From the point of view of customers, if an employee wears the company logo or answers their calls or opens the door for them, that employee is *your* employee.

To make matters much worse, so many of these subcontractings-gone-wrong happen at hellos and good-byes. The rationales do not help: *"Oh, he works for the security company"*; *"Oh, they're the parking subcontractor"*; or *"I'm sorry she barked at you on the phone—she's a temp."*

In essence, such statements are a way of coaxing customers (or yourself) to accept the idea that *"that* is not *us."* To your customers, such statements are just infuriating baloney. "If I buy a product from you," explained one such customer, "and it's serviced by somebody else you hired, well, I'm sorry; to me that's *your* service." And if that rough service happens at an entry or exit point, it is harming a critical, emotion-filled moment that has a strong hand in shaping your customer's perception of your brand.

When a Botched Welcome Isn't Your Fault, You Still Need to Fix It

A botched hello or good-bye can occur in spite of your best intentions. Your staff still needs to recognize and address it—before it colors the customer's entire experience. Hospitality veteran Jay Coldren tells of an incident that made an impression on him early in his career. Jay had recently started as a manager at a well-known country inn and restaurant when a couple from Pittsburgh drove up for a three-night stay to celebrate their twenty-fifth anniversary. The trip had been arranged a year in advance; the couple had read the chef's cookbook together before they set out; waxed up their car so they would arrive in style; even packed up a special picnic to enjoy on the four hour drive. Together they had enjoyed scheduling nearly every last minute of how they expected to spend their visit. But unfortunately . . .

As the staff unloaded the luggage, our female guest said to her husband, "Don't forget my hanging bag." Her husband looked into the trunk and came up with a horrified expression on his face. Apparently, she had left her bag beside the car in their garage assuming he would pack it, but he never saw it. At this point, she pretty much fell apart:

This poor woman was checking into one of the most expensive places on the planet with nothing but the clothes on her back! As the doormen and I tried to figure out what to do to make this couple happy, one of the staff who had been there a lot longer than me drove up to the front of the inn in the company car. I looked at him oddly and he just smiled and said, "Get me their keys and the address; I'll be back before dinner." I was floored. No one asked him to do this, and there wasn't a moment's hesitation on his part. He was so much a part of the service culture that he just knew the exact right thing to do. He was halfway to Pittsburgh before the lady actually believed that we were really going to get her luggage at her house. He drove eight hours straight and made it back before their dinner reservations at nine.[4]

Good-Bye for Now from the Authors—with Resources and Assistance for Your Journey

Good-bye is your last—and perhaps your most memorable—chance to add a final brush stroke to the fresco of customer experience. It's important to make it count. And as we add our last stroke to your experience with this book, we want to let you know how grateful we are that you have spent this time with us.

We encourage you to contact us on any subject we have covered or that you feel you'd like to have covered more thoroughly; we are always pleased to hear from you.

Leonardo can be reached at Linghilleri@westpacesconsulting.com. His consulting firm's tag line is "Architects of Legendary Customer Service," and he awaits the next challenge to fulfill his firm's brand promise.

Micah is most quickly reached at micah@micahsolomon.com. Also on this website (www.micahsolomon.com) are the photographs and additional narrative examples related to this book and these subjects that we think you'll find helpful.

Thank you again for spending this time with us, and best wishes for providing exceptional, loyalty-building service.

Appendixes

We would like to offer you some specific examples of real-world communication to employees about service standards and company philosophy. Here are three concrete examples of the way a company's staff can be encouraged to anticipate the needs of their customers. Each was crafted for the company's individual situation and the special relationship it has with its customers. We hope that these examples will spark your own explorations into the art of anticipation.

The *Oasis Disc Manufacturing Customer and Phone Interaction Guidelines and Lexicon Excerpts* demonstrate telephone and in-person customer interaction guidelines, language choice pointers, and general principles in abbreviated form. It is for use by employees with direct contact with the public. This example shows how our principles apply to Micah's business, Oasis, a relatively informal company. It is of an appropriate length to form a tri-fold brochure for easy workplace reference and to be excerpted for even readier reference in pocket form.

The *Capella Hotels and Resorts "Canon Card"/Service Standards and Operating Philosophy* illustrates how a luxury organization with a relatively formal service style distills its service standards and operating philosophy into a brief, portable set of instructions and examples. The card that they're printed on is small enough to accordion-fold and carry in one's pocket. These principles and action points can keep employees focused on their overall purpose in the organization (the Canon side of the brochure) and the key steps/building blocks for different situations that involve working with customers and with other employees (the Service Standards side).

The *CARQUEST Standards of Service Excellence* is the most concise and least formal example we have provided. It shows how a brief, portable set of principles and action points can be transformative for a company within an informal customer relations context. It is short enough to post at various locations in a workplace.

The copyrights for the appendixes are as follows:

Appendix A: © Four Aces Inc., courtesy of Micah Solomon, All Rights Reserved

Appendix B: © General Parts, Inc., All Rights Reserved

Appendix C: © West Paces Hotel Group, All Rights Reserved

Oasis Disc Manufacturing: Customer and Phone Interaction Guidelines and Lexicon Excerpts

© Four Aces Inc. All Rights Reserved, Courtesy Micah Solomon

Customer Interaction Guidelines

- **Preferred acknowledgements and greetings**

  - "Absolutely"
  - "I'll be happy to"
  - "Right away!"
  - "It will be my pleasure"
  - "My pleasure"
  - "Thank YOU!"
  - You are very welcome!
  - You're welcome.
  - Good Morning/Afternoon/Evening
  - You bet! (but don't over-use!)

- **Discouraged acknowledgments and greetings:**

  - No problem! (this is appropriate only when you are trying to convince a customer that they truly haven't inconvenienced you)
  - OK!
  - Hi.

  Unacceptable acknowledgments and greetings:

  - Sure.
  - Uh huh (and other similar vocalizations)
  - Yes? (as a response to a comment by a customer like "Hi. This is Jerry Customer.")

- **There are dozens of better and worse ways to use language.**
  MANY times it's truly "not what you say but how you say it." Keep this in mind and choose your words carefully.

  Examples of good and bad language:
  - Not acceptable: "you owe..."
  - Good: "our records show a balance of..." (note: rough collection methods are an EASY way to lose customers).

  - Not acceptable: "You need to..."
  - Good: "We find it works best if you..."

- **Answering the telephone (external calls):**
  - Welcome to Oasis, this is (name), how may I assist you?
  - Thank you for calling Oasis, this is (name), how may I help you?"
  - Oasis--good morning, this is (name) how may I assist you?
  - Oasis--good morning. May I please place you on a brief hold? (caller is in control)

  (If you are going to use time-specific greetings, be sure you can get it right not answer "good morning" at 1 PM or "good afternoon" at 10 AM!)

- **Answering the telephone (internal calls):**
  - Reception, this is (name), how may I assist you?
  - Reception, May I please place you on a brief hold?

- **Apologies:**

  - I am so sorry you experienced this problem, please forgive us. What can I do to assist you and make it right?
  - I am sorry to hear that, please forgive us! Let me attempt to correct this issue right away......
  - I am terribly sorry, please forgive us. What can I do to help?
  - I am sorry to hear that, how can I help?

- **Pleasant Departure:**

  - Have a wonderful day, good-bye
  - Thank you for working with us today
  - Thank you for calling Oasis, good-bye

Telephone Interaction Guidelines

Key Concepts:
- Calling Oasis is a pleasant experience for the caller that adds value for the caller.
- External callers should always experience a three-element response:
  1. *A pleasant greeting*
  2. *A self identification (identify Oasis and the person answering the phone)*
  3. *An offer of assistance*
- The interaction with the caller should be warm, sincere and spirited (full of character)
- We always adjust and conform to the pace of the caller
- Oasis' preferred terminology should be used at all times. However, each person can choose his or her greetings within the guidelines
- Once we are aware of the name of the caller, we use it when possible, within reason. (But do not extend this too far beyond what would be natural in everyday speech.)
- The caller is always in control of the phone conversation.
- Every call is ended with a warm farewell and the use of the caller's name, if possible.
- Internal call standards are consistent (but not identical) with external calls:
  - *Internal callers should experience, at minimum, a self-identification and a greeting, or a self-identification and an offer of assistance. For example.: Good morning, this is Steven! or: This is Steven, how may I help you? Or simply "Hello, this is Steven."*

- **Example 1: (Caller in italics)**
  - Welcome to Oasis, this is Michelle, how may I help you?
  - *Hi. I'd like to speak with Jane…*
  - Absolutely! I'm happy to connect you. While I'm connecting you would you mind if I check your customer information so that we're sure your profile is up to date?
  - *No prob.*
  - [CSR prompts caller to update file]
  - Thank you for helping me with that! Please hold…. (CSR informs Jane that she has a call) Mr. ____, go ahead please.
  - *Thank you!*
  - You're welcome! (Operator disconnects)

- **Example 2: (Caller in italics)**
  - Thank you for calling Oasis, this is Penny, how may I assist you?
  - *Hey, this is Bill Smith, I'd like to speak with Marty….*
  - You bet! I am happy to connect you. While I'm connecting you would you mind if I check your customer information so that we're sure your profile is up to date?
  - *No, I just want to talk with Marty!*
  - Absolutely, Bill! (Operator does not find Marty)
  - I am so sorry, Marty is not answering his line, may I offer you his voice mail?
  - *Can you just tell him to call me at 404 555 1212.*
  - Absolutely. I'll put the message where I know he'll get it. Is there anything else I can do for you?
  - *I'm good, thanks.*
  - You're welcome, Bill… have a wonderful day!

- **The caller is always in control:**
  - No surprises! (e.g. automatic transfer to empty line/voicemail)
  - Agrees to be placed on hold (except momentary hold for connection)
  - No extensive holding of the line (1 minute max without explicit permission)

Call screening, if any, must be done in a way that is completely hidden from the caller.
Never ever ever say "and the purpose of this call is?" "who are you with?" "Will she know what you're calling about?" or other insulting questions. Instead prompt for info as scripted on page 3, or in a faster situation say "You bet--may I get your name so I can pass it on to him?"

(Note how this brief, invisible screening includes both a request AND the reason for this request, and the reason must clearly not be that he or she is screening calls).

(NOTE--this is a KEY point. Customers despise having their calls screened, so this wording is critical. You need to give them the feeling that they ALREADY have made it through the screening process BEFORE they are asked to divulge their names; the info you ask for must be requested for professional purposes, not to get them past the velvet rope.)

No speaker phone (unless agreed upon)
Wait until the caller hangs up before disconnecting
Always have "the last word" (e.g., as follows): Caller's in *italics:*
- Thank you for calling Oasis! This is Steven. How may I assist you?
- *Good Morning...*
- Good morning Steven!
- *.....Could you please connect me with Jerry Seinfeld?*
- I will be happy to! Please hold.
- *Thank you!*
- You are welcome! .....Jerry is on the line, please go ahead.
- *Thank you!*
- You are very welcome!

Pointers and Pet Peeves

- **How you answer the query "how are you" and "how are you doing?" may set the tone for your entire interaction.**
    - Always respond to "how are you?" with both an answer as to how you're doing and a query as to how your client is doing. Obviously this is part of the principle to "always have the last word," but it is such a key point that it is restated here.
    - If asked, always answer with an unequivocally positive response as to how you're doing. "I'm doing great!" or "Wonderful" or "Super" or something similarly cheery.* The only, rare exception to this is if something truly bad has happened to you and you know the client personally and it seems appropriate to discuss.
        ("I'm well" can sound a bit too perfect and make a client subliminally uneasy in our informal business.)

- **Use the following precise wording when transferring to voicemail:** "May I offer you her voicemail?" Also note that some people HATE to be transferred to voicemail. For this reason also consider creative options such as offering to "hand-carry a message to her when she comes back to the office."

- **Once you have a client on hold: make sure you check back regularly.** If possible, gently encourage client to go into voicemail. If the client insists on holding, apologize for the delay, even if you feel the client is being stubborn. NOTE: Oasis is small. We are mobile. If a note waved in front of someone's face or an IM to someone in an other office is what's called for, go for it!

- **Oasis has very few "policies" that are unchangeable. (And "policy" is a word you should never use with a client.)** If you find yourself quoting policy and getting more and more inflexible until you're backed into a corner, slow down, breathe, and call for backup.

- **Oasis people are not snobs.**
    - We use carefully-chosen language in our scripts only to improve the customer interaction, never to be snooty or excessively formal.
    - We avoid pre-judging people negatively based on superficial impressions. In the music business, it is hard to tell who is "important" and who is not, so we assume everyone has importance to Oasis.

- **Try to avoid the word "No."**
    - Even if you're giving a client the definitive (negative) answer, there's almost always a way to soften the blow: "That's an interesting idea; however we have a method in place that we find works really well for us. May I go over it with you?" When "no" is the final answer, offering an alternative solution and apology makes it easier to accept: "I'm sorry, Mr. Jamison, although we were unable to upgrade the shipping of your complete project to Madagascar for free, would it help if we ship two boxes overnight at our expense?" (long story short: don't say the "no" without having a "yes" within the same breath.)

- **Check your voicemail and email.**
    - The only excuse for not checking your voicemail is if you're involved in some difficult "think" project that requires all your concentration. (This is also one of the only excuses for letting a call go to voicemail in the first place.) When you cannot be in the office, leave an alternate greeting on the phone that addresses this--or check your voicemail frequently during your absence.

    - **In your outgoing voicemail message or when leaving voicemails for other, don't speed up when you're saying the digits:** say any numbers or unusual name spellings slowly and always be sure to repeat them! People should be able to write these tidbits down ideally without rewinding the tape or calling back to hear your announcement a second time.

- **There are technical skills involved in using the phone. Learn them!**
- **Last names, extension numbers (or direct dial numbers) and email addresses are "musts":** use them in your voicemails and emails to make it easy for a client to call you back.

- **Nothing in this document should preclude you from being "real people" on the phone** or even becoming real friends with your clients and prospective clients (assuming you remain protective of Oasis interests).
- **We aren't just selling a product. We are paying attention: to our clients, their music and their aspirations.** Showing genuine interest in the client's project is one of the most important parts of your job.

- **If a client or prospect is being rude, always stay polite.**
  - There are those people who are naturally rude (and your attitude won't change that) and those who are so upset they've become rude as a last resort (in which case your attitude can make a world of difference). Remember: stay polite. It's not fair, but it's the way it MUST be at Oasis.
- **Even if in public the Oasis customer is always supported, know that you're supported behind the scenes.**
  - Sometimes Oasis has to apologize for things that truly aren't our/your fault--don't think that management doesn't understand this.

Never embarrass or contradict a customer.

  - If they get very angry over something, it is quite likely the next day they will feel badly about how they acted.
  - If they make a mistake, don't point it out to them unless it's absolutely necessary. And then make it seem like an easy mistake that anyone could have made.

CARQUEST Standards of Service Excellence

© General Parts, Inc. All Rights Reserved

Standards of Service Excellence

Our Motto:
Exceptional Teammates Proudly Serving a World in Motion

Our Ambition:
Providing unparalleled customer service, innovation, teammate opportunities and industry leadership

Our Promise:
A Passion for Excellence

"A Passion to Serve"

© Copyright 2007, CARQUEST Corporation

Our Standards of Service Excellence

- Providing unparalleled service is my personal role and the focus of our team efforts.

- I build and sustain customer trust by always demonstrating that I care.

- I am responsible for the cleanliness of our stores, facilities, work areas and vehicles. My appearance, behavior and language reflect our brand of excellence.

- When I see a problem I own it until it is resolved. I am empowered to ensure customer satisfaction and loyalty.

- I build relationships that create customers for life.

- I embrace and foster diversity in teammates and customers.

- I am always eager to assist my teammates by stepping out of my primary role to serve our customers.

- I always conduct myself with strong character and integrity in protecting and elevating the Company name and reputation.

- I am always gracious and treat customers and teammates with dignity and respect.

- I enjoy what I do. I have a warm, happy and caring attitude that creates a pleasant customer experience.

- I am responsible for the safety of my teammates and customers. I conduct myself safely and responsibly in the community I serve.

- I am trained and knowledgeable to provide excellent service to our customers.

- I am prompt, reliable, and responsive. I complete my commitments on time, showing dedication and professionalism. I go beyond my customers' expectations.

- I am a leader. I lead by example and I am a role model at work and in the community. I operate with uncompromising values.

Capella Hotels and Resorts "Canon Card": Service Standards and Operating Philosophy

© West Paces Hotel Group, All Rights Reserved

CANON

The West Paces Hotel Group is in business to create value and unparalleled results for our owners by creating products which fulfill individual customer expectations.

We deliver reliable, genuinely caring and timely service superior to our competition, with respected and empowered employees who work in an environment of belonging and purpose.

We are supportive and contributing members of society, operating with uncompromising values, honor and integrity.

CAPELLA™
HOTELS AND RESORTS

ZEITGEIST
"The Spirit of the Moment"

We, the Service Professionals of Capella place our guests at the center of everything we do. We provide.

EXCLUSIVITY
A unique, private and luxurious environment that creates a sense of belonging where our guests and residents feel at ease

LOYALTY
Unobtrusive, gracious and unscripted service which enables and empowers our guests and residents to define and fulfill their individual experience

EXPERIENCE
Connections with the local culture and an array of activities along with friendly, respectful, caring and personalized service that is perfectly timed and defect-free

LEGACY
Memories that are meaningful and enriching extending beyond the stay of our guests and residents

VISION
We are the Global Leader in the service business. Our accomplishments and meaningful contributions have a positive impact on society

MISSION
Our brands, our independent hotels, and our other businesses are recognized as the undisputed leaders in their respective market segments

OBJECTIVES
Keep our existing customers
Add new customers
Optimize the spend of each customer
Maximize efficiency in our service delivery

SERVICE PROCESS
1. WARM WELCOME
Eye contact and smile
Observe
Greet by name whenever possible
2. COMPLIANCE AND ANTICIPATION OF GUESTS' NEEDS
Engage and adjust to the pace of the guest
Fulfill expected and expressed needs
Anticipate
Ask if any other assistance is needed
3. FOND FAREWELL

SERVICE STANDARDS

1. The Canon states the purpose for us to be in business and is shared within the organization.

2. The Zeitgeist is known, owned, and energized by all. It is the cornerstone of our service commitment to our guests.

3. Our Service Process is followed for all guest interactions.

4. We assist each other, stepping out of our primary duties to effectively provide service to our guests.

5. Answer the telephone within three rings and with a smile in your voice. Use terminology that reflects Capella's image. Do not screen calls. Avoid call transfers and placing guests on hold.

6. You are responsible to identify and immediately correct defects before they affect a guest. Defect prevention is key to service excellence.

7. Ensure all areas of the hotel are immaculate. We are responsible for cleanliness, maintenance, and organization. Each hotel follows our established CARE program.

8. Always recognize guests. Interrupt whatever activity you are doing when a guest is within 3 meters (12 feet); greet them with a smile and offer assistance.

9. Safety and security is everyone's responsibility. Know your role in an emergency situation and in protecting guest and hotel assets. Report unsafe conditions or security concerns immediately and correct them if possible.

10. We are all responsible to participate in the elimination of defects in our work area for continuous improvement.

11. When a guest encounters any difficulty, you are responsible to own it and start the problem resolution process. You are empowered to resolve any problem to the guest's complete satisfaction. Follow the OIAF process to properly document issues.

12. Escort guests until they are comfortable with the directions or make visual contact with their destination. Do not point.

13. Always give guests your complete attention and focus. Be responsive, caring and timely in providing service.

14. Be respectful of our guests' personal time and privacy, delivering service that does not interrupt or interfere with our guests' activities. Never approach a guest to request a favor, such as an autograph.

15. The Capella experience is memorable and unique. Be proactive, finding ways to surprise and delight our guests.

16. Be sensitive and adjust to the guests' style, pace, situation and each unique environment to create a personal experience for them.

17. Our appearance, grooming, and demeanor represent Capella. Our attire and personal image are appropriate and impeccable. We avoid words that are inconsistent with Capella's image, such as "hi", "ok", "no problem", "guys", etc.

18. The suggested hours of operation are guidelines, not limitations for satisfying individual guest desires and preferences.

19. We are empowered and required to fulfill our guests' needs. Identify their unique requirements and preferences both prior to the arrival and during their stay in order to individualize their experience.

20. Knowledge is essential to create the Capella experience for our guests. Know all hotel services and signature activities along with local features, history, and traditions.

21. Confidentiality at Capella is paramount. Never speak to the press or anyone outside our company concerning the hotel and guests. If you are approached for information, please notify your General Manager.

22. Be positive both inside and outside the workplace. It is our responsibility to create a great environment and reputation for our hotel and each other.

23. All forms of our written communication (signage, letters, e-mail, hand written notes, etc.) reflect Capella's image.

24. As service professionals, we are always gracious and treat our guests and each other with respect and dignity.

Notes

Chapter Three

1. For more on Danny Meyer's approach to hospitality (the term he prefers to "service"), we recommend his *Setting The Table: The Transforming Power of Hospitality in Business*, HarperCollins, New York, 2006.

2. Elizabeth Loftus, *Memory*, Ardsley House, New York, 1980, pp 24–25.

3. Phoebe Damrosch, *Service Included: Four-Star Secrets of an Eavesdropping Waiter*, William Morrow, New York, 2007.

4. *New York Times*, September 24, 2007: "Walmart.com to Customers: Stop Calling."

Chapter Five

1. Gary Heil, Tom Parker, Deborah C. Stephens, *One Size Fits One*, Wiley, New York, 1999, p 43.

2. *Harvard Business Review*, March 2006.

3. *Seth's Blog* entry, December 11, 2007, www.sethgodin.com

Chapter Six

1. Bill Bryson, *A Walk In The Woods*, Broadway Books, 1999.

2. Edmund Lawler: *Lessons in Service from Charlie Trotter*, Ten Speed Press, Berkeley, CA, 2001.

3. A caution: Such changes should be made carefully, intelligently, and flexibly. The routines of the professional kitchen—like other artisanal environments—have developed over centuries. Thousands of subtle details and "tradeskills" are embedded in the traditional kitchen's routines, and in those who have apprenticed in them. When applying a modern manufacturing-based approach to such an environment, the unique advantages of the artisanal traditions must be preserved along with the advantages of the new ways you bring in. This kind of integration requires a soft touch.

Chapter Seven

1. Martin E. P. Seligman, PhD, *Learned Optimism: How to Change Your Mind and Your Life,* Free Press, NY, 1998, p 257.

Chapter Nine

1. Carl Sewell and Paul B. Brown, *Customers for Life: How to Turn That One-Time Buyer into a Lifetime Customer,* Broadway Business, Revised ed., 2002, p 13.

Chapter Ten

1. http://www.wired.com/techbiz/it/magazine/16-03/ff_free

2. *Keyboard,* December 1, 2008.

3. Mark Penn and E. Kinney Zalesne, *Just 1%: The Power of Microtrends*, Change This, Milwaukee, WI, 2007, p 8. Viewable at www.changethis.com.

4. *New York Times,* "At Netflix, Victory for Voices Over Keystrokes," August 16, 2007.

5. CD Baby confirmation letter as of April 2009.

6. Henry David Thoreau, *Walden; or, Life in the Woods,* Ticknor and Fields, Boston, 1854.

7. Seth Godin, *Seth's Blog,* January 31, 2008. Longer and much-worth reading discussion in his book *Permission Marketing,* Simon & Schuster, New York, 1999.

8. Amazon.com CTO Werner Vogel's blog entry, http://www.all thingsdistributed.com/2006/06/you_guard_it_with_your_life.html

9. http://www.joystiq.com/2008/05/06/wii-fit-sells-out-on-amazon-2-5-units-sold-every-minute/

Chapter Eleven

1. Elizabeth Loftus, *Memory,* pp 24–25 .

2. *The Odyssey,* Homer, translated by Robert Fagles, introduction by Bernard Knox, Penguin Classics, New York, 1996.

3. Danny Meyer, *Setting The Table,* p 215.

4. Personal Courtesy of Jay Coldren, December 2007.

Index